TO HAVE... a body
family
church
government
neighbors
intellect
money
talents
Bible
food
clothing
water
breath
eyes
ears
voice
love
radio
television
telephone
peace
forgiveness
hope
eternal life
car
country
doctors
college
laws
Jesus **...IS TO OWE**

"I AM DEBTOR"

Life is a gem
of worth so rare,
he who has it
is millionaire.

To have it, though,
is not to own;
life is merely
a short-term loan.

That I should act
as though I own
my earthly life--
I, I alone--

and wear the gem
for show, and fife
my self's import
and pride of life;

or play with the gem
like boys with marbles,
its priceless worth
with marbles garble;

or hide away
the jewel stone,
withdraw from crowds
and live alone--

forbid it, Lord!
Help me instead
to share myself,
wy wealth, my bread,

my love, my care
with fellowmen.
This is my prayer!
Amen! Amen!

TO HAVE IS TO OWE

Norman A. Wingert

Bunkhouse Publishers, Inc.
123 North Sultana
Ontario, California

Cover illustration by
Cathy Jones

Norman A. Wingert
TO HAVE IS TO OWE

ISBN 0-937594-00-8

Printed in United States of America

Philippians 4:8
"...if there be any virtue and if
there be any praise, think on these
things," and if you like, use them.

DEDICATION

To have...

Eunice
Lois and Robert
Norman O. and Marie
Raymond
Rena
David
Ronnie
Debby
Ryan
and Robyn

...is to owe

—Norman A.

MINI BIOGRAPHY OF AUTHOR

1. Birth through High School, Chambersburg, Pennsylvania 1898-1917

2. Two-year course in Bible, Messiah Bible School, Pennsylvania 1918-1920

3. College (Litt.B. and M.A.) 1921-1926
   - One year Messiah College
   - Four years Grove City College

4. Employment in Chicago 1926-1927
   - Illinois Children's Home and Aid Society
   - Remington Typewriter Company

5. Teaching 1928-1948
   - Jabbok Bible School, Oklahoma 1928-1930
   - Southwestern Teachers College, Oklahoma 1930-1931
   - Messiah College, Pennsylvania 1932-1942
   - Upland College, California 1945-1948

6. Relief Work: Mennonite Central Committee 1948-1970
   - Germany 1948-1949
   - Austria 1950-1952
   - Japan 1953-1957
   - Hong Kong 1958-1960
   - Burundi, Africa 1962-1964
   - Reedley, California 1964-1970

7. Retirement 1970-
   - Round-the-world writing mission
   - Return to Burundi on our own after the tribal war there
   - Books Published:
     - "No Place to Stop Killing"
     - "Why Idi Amin? A Christian Perspective"
     - "To Have Is to Owe"

FOREWORD

This book might well be called a Wingert Miscellany of certain incidents, observations and convictions that have appeared in print previously and of writings that have been born since our retirement. The stories and reflections come out of a quarter century of relief work on four continents.*

Rather than a treatise that must be developed with scholarly expertise, the volume is more like a long personal letter with probably too little attention to editorial niceties. I am eager that the book, which may prove to be the swan song of an octogenarian, convey the joy and gratefulness Eunice, my wife, and I feel for the opportunity that God and Mennonite Central Committee have granted us to serve the needy and suffering peoples around the world.

These years have left two deep convictions which are reflected repeatedly within the covers of this book. The first one is that of the ever-widening chasm between the Haves and the Have-nots in the world, and the second one is the primacy of Jesus Christ and the biblical imperative for Christian social concern.

Regarding the contrast in levels of living, I saw one day in Bujumbura, Burundi, a raggedly dressed little girl going about in the town market with an orange in her hand offering it for sale for five Burundi francs. Since oranges are a luxury item in Burundi, where the average personal income is less than $40 a year, the undernourished girl was no doubt intending to buy a more substantial food befitting her lifestyle of eating just to stay alive. Is it to be wondered at that Eunice and I have been feeling uncomfortable now that we are again being pressed into the mold of the comfortable American good life!

For a contrasting level of living, observe an American businessman as he draws up to an average motel in an average American village. He unpacks his wardrobe, soaks and relaxes in a tub of sudsy hot water or a copious shower, dries himself with three soft towels, crawls into his boxspring mattress bed or waterbed, turns on the color television, sends his love a thousand miles to his family via the bedside telephone, drops a quarter into the slot to be rocked to sleep by his massaging bed, turns off the dome and bedside lights, but doesn't bother about the bathroom lights. "Anyway," he says by his casualness, "isn't it the way Americans do?"

It is this gulf between "them" and "us" that gives us concern. For years we lived among homeless and hungry people, and now that our new-made friends came along home with us, the feeling of injustice continues. Sometimes their saucer-eyed, gaunt-bodied ghosts take chairs opposite us at our laden dinner table. We would be enjoying the American good life more had not the Mennonite Central Committee planted us into that faraway world.

The second main reason for the writing of this book has to do with the spiritual. Beyond the food and the clothing, the medicines and the expertise training, there are areas where human help cannot go. How pitiful, then, if the Christian, who knows where superhuman help lies, does not point the needy to that Source and thus supplement his own effort and that of his organization with the mercies of our All-powerful and All-loving God! The structured evils of the world community, like individual wrongdoing, bespeak the inherent greed and selfishness of the human heart and call for a dynamic beyond the humanitarian.

The basic tenet of the churches supporting the Mennonite Central Committee and other evangelical relief organizations proclaims that Jesus Christ is "the Way, the Truth and the Life," and that a personal confession of faith in Him is rewarded by the assurance of eternal life, an assurance that can bring peace in the direst of circumstances. Medical doctors and psychiatrists concur that this inner rightness with God is essential to the complete wholeness and restoration of the hurt and hurting individual. Material relief and spiritual aid are, indeed, complementary and should go hand in hand for the Christian social worker.

A final word. At 80 and 82, Eunice and I find ourselves indebted to so many friends that a declaration of bankruptcy is our only course of action: the friendships forged overseas; the hospitalities received in a thousand deputational programs across the United States and Canada; the passing contacts experienced in a three-time circling of the earth; our brothers and sisters in the Lord in our home congregations; and especially the MCC administrators and fellow workers around the world. We greet you all warmly, all you who read this page. Do carry on while we relinquish the reins. We're getting to feel ourselves Model T Fords on life's highway. As you whiz by, we bid you note the signs on our old jalopy, "God Bless You!" both fore and aft. And when you come to the crossroads of life (cloverleafs) and are faced with decisions, do remember that *to have is not to own, but to owe.*

---

*See the "Minibiography" on page viii

The "Contents" which follow may seem to lack an orderly subject and chronological arrangement. Largely, this scrapbookish form is so intended. The alternating stories of differing locale and situations give one a sense of the universality of human nature and human suffering. Spiritual emphases and personal convictions add to the impression of the book as a Miscellany.

CONTENTS

I - Poverty, Affluence and Servanthood

II - Mennonite Central Committee

III - Miscellaneous

IV - Beyond Human Help -- CHRIST

V - Poems

I

POVERTY
AFFLUENCE
and
SERVANTHOOD

PEOPLE IN ALL KINDS OF TROUBLES

During our nearly thirteen years of relief work overseas, we had to do with people; hungry people, suffering people, people who love and hate and hope and cry and die. Can one, like Nero, fiddle while Rome burns? "The harvest is great, but the laborers few." We got up one morning in Hong Kong to find a Chinese refugee woman had given birth to a baby at the bottom of our stairwell during the night. Two once wealthy Mennonite refugees from the Ukraine came to Kiel, Germany, in dresses that were patch upon patch. "We never thought this could happen to *us*," they said. A twelve-year-old girl came to our clothing center in Vienna, Austria, alone; she said she had seen her parents blown to bits when they tripped a border mine. On Christmas Day, 1958, I distributed bundles of clothing to over 200 lepers; lepers are people, you know! Eunice met a Jewess in Switzerland who saw her parents burned in Hitler's ovens. She had to carry wood for those ovens, but escaped before it came her turn. For 30 days I hosted 40 teen-age young men, most of whom were Hitler's soldiers who had just returned from prison camps in Russia. When they got to Kiel, Germany, they found their homes bombed and their families killed. Imagine living for thirty days with young, bruised personalities such as these! A mother in Bujumbura, Burundi, asked me for a box or carton in which to bury her baby which had just died. She was crying, for she loved her baby. I visited a refugee school in the Burundi hills so poor they used their black bodies for slates and green tree twigs for chalk. The pupils had felled trees for seats and the teacher had a tree stump for her desk. We had occasional distributions of clothing for boat people around Hong Kong, the poorest of the poor. They live their lives from birth to death on their sampans. Boat women at the Kwong Wah Charity Hospital's maternity ward begged Eunice to take their babies; they just could not afford to feed another mouth.

We can continue telling of these sufferings and tragedies of humankind which it has been our lot to meet with firsthand. But we've seen more than sufferings and tragedies; we've also seen the grace of God at work in many of these same people. If we've heard dirges and groans and moans, we've also heard notes of joy and victory. Indeed, we've seen such marvelous spiritual victories over adverse circumstances that it almost makes us want to pray for hardships so that we may experience the power in our lives that comes through suffering. The story of my visit to Lillian Dickson's Leprosarium in Taiwan illustrates well what I mean.

God helps us in all our troubles, so that we are able to help others who have all kinds of troubles, using the same help that we ourselves have received from God.

-II Corinthians 1:4, The Good News Bible-

THE ACCORDIONIST

Somewhere someone is playing "Home Sweet Home" on an accordion. He plays slowly, beautifully, feelingly. I am sure he must be a refugee from the Mainland. Every evening at dusk he plays it over and over and over again. I can hear him above the hubbub of the rabble below through my third-floor open window, for in April it is already warm in Hong Kong.

I have a strong feeling the tune is the magic carpet that transports him back to the home of his happier days. The way he plays it tells me that. And although he plays it for his own heart, I think he must at the same time be interpreting the homesickness of the million refugees in Hong Kong who, too, have left friends and homes behind them.

What a crescendo of plaint ascends to heaven from Hong Kong and from other lands of God's fair earth! At no time in world history have there been so many people who have had to leave where they wanted to be and go to places where they weren't wanted. Homesickness has become a universal ache. The Chinese accordionist is expressing the heartthrobs of all the world's homeless everywhere and not only of those in Hong Kong.

But the accordionist knows Hong Kong's millions best, for he was one of them in the south-flowing stream. Hong Kong is a dam that must constantly build its dikes higher. In other lands refugees are siphoned off from the camps, but here there is no farther place for them to go, and there are areas with 2000 persons to the acre. Families live in lean-to shacks or hallways or rooftops of other buildings, or in cement cubicles which the Colony has put up for them. And still the stream flows and the dam deepens and the United Nations has recognized Hong Kong to be the densest refugee-populated spot on earth.

The accordionist has finally stopped playing "Home Sweet Home." Tomorrow evening he will play again.

GIFT BUNDLES FOR LEPROSY PATIENTS

Eleven days before Christmas, 1962, in New York harbor, seventeen big oil drums filled with more than a thousand towel-wrapped gift bundles for leprosy patients were stashed in the hold of the steamship "Africa Moon." By the name of the vessel one could, of course, know that the gifts would not reach journey's end in time for Christmas giving.

Across the Atlantic sailed the "Africa Moon," then into the Mediterranean and through the Suez Canal and the Red Sea, and finally, halfway down the east coast of Africa to Dar-es-Salaam, one of the coastal cities of Tanganyika. At Dar-es-Salaam deck planks were taken up and the drums transferred to an East African Railroad freight car. For nearly a week the train rattled along westward until it was stopped by 400-mile long Lake Tanganyika at about its midpoint, a little place called Kigoma. Here it was back to ship again; the drums were loaded onto a barge for forty-eight hours of sailing northward to Usumbura (later, Bujumbura) at the head of the lake. Usumbura is the capital of the newly-independent Kingdom of Burundi, in the very heart of Africa. It took exactly two months for the shipment to make the sea-land-lake journey from New York to Usumbura.

But this was still not journey's end. After three weeks in a warehouse, the drums were loaded onto a truck for the last leg of their long journey. Up went the truck over very rough and curving roads from the lake level to the high tablelands of central Africa, and 125 miles later, there came into view a triangular bed of red flag flowers, and on one corner a sign in French spelling, "Leproserie Nyankanda." Here, at last, was journey's end.

Here nearly 700 African leprosy patients are living in grass huts clustered around a dozen western-style buildings. Take away the hospital and its patients, and Nyankanda would be a name only, an empty spot like the sparsely populated country round about. This largely uncultivated "bush" land has been, and to some extent still is, the habitat for lions and leopards, hippos and boas, buffaloes and monkeys. The lonely cowpath road past the hospital plays hide-and-seek with itself as it winds up and down, around and between the hills and knobs and truncated cones that project out of nearly 7,000-foot-elevated tableland.

For these simple, largely unlettered, but friendly leprosy patients, life is grimly circumscribed and severe. Usumbura is so far away it is an unimaginable world. The few who have been there were amazed at the sight of the big lake and of the apartment houses (people actually living on top of others!). Had one the power to describe vividly enough in words the clothing they and all poorer Africans wear, Americans would hardly believe it. The arrival of these gift bundles was therefore for them an event to be remembered.

It was Sunday afternoon, March 10, 1963. Leprosy patients and their families surrounded the big Protestant church. They had come early. Inside, the hospital personnel were working feverishly, laying out the colorful gift bundles in different piles to facilitate distribution. Outside, old and young alike were on tiptoe (those who had toes), craning their necks to see through windows and partly barred doors what was going on inside. When the doors were opened fifteen minutes past schedule, the church filled in no time at all, but it took fifteen more minutes for the excitement to subside and the program to begin. They sang several Christian songs to the beating of the church drums. Whose emotions would not be stirred in looking down on a congregation of 1,000 African people, nearly 700 of whom were afflicted with the disease of leprosy, many of them deformed in face and foot and finger!

The speaker began: "In a country far away, there are Christian people who know about you and pray for you and wish you well. They send you greetings, and they have sent with their greetings the gifts which you see here at the front of the church and they want to share these things with you."

The interpreter had to interrupt the speaker frequently to keep order; so excited were the people that they kept pressing forward toward the piles of bundles.

The speaker continued: "Before you go to sleep tonight, will you pray to God and thank Him for your gift, thank Him for putting it into the hearts of Christians to show you this kindness? And how can you show your thanks? By passing on a kindness to someone else, even if it is only a smile." The audience was listening attentively.

The tension reached its highest point when the speaker picked up one of the safety-pinned towels, called a little girl leprosy patient to the platform, opened the bundle and handed the timid but smiling girl its precious contents, item by item. The audience burst into spontaneous applause.

Then began the name-calling. Hospital personnel had prepared lists of all the patients, and each was to come forward when he heard his name read. The space between the bundles and the people had to be cleared repeatedly, so persistently did the expectant recipients keep pressing forward. As each received his bundle he made his exit through a side door to the church yard to see what was inside his towel.

The drama continued for several hours. Gradually the crowd inside grew less and the crowd outside increased.

What an experience! There they came, women, men, children! Some hobbled on partly-eaten feet, some had dropfoot, others who were in a more advanced stage used crutches. A few of the reaching hands had no fingers. There were disfigured faces, twisted mouths, missing noses. Happily, there were many who showed no visible signs of the disease. But whether there were marks or not, all those who were filing past the receiving stand were victims of that dreaded disease which society over the centuries has chosen to designate as "The Unclean."

It was a joy to give them some new things that normal people like, and not just castaway items that normal people have finished with. These people are not untouchables; they are human beings, warm, friendly, thankful!

After the main distribution, bundles were carried into the wards for those who could not walk. "This is my pride and joy," said the nurse as she pointed to a disfigured but broadly-smiling girl; even here happiness and hope are not unknown.

The resident doctor said, "Those who have been workers here through the years say that never before has there been a distribution of gifts like this."

So the long sea-land-lake journey of the drums seems not to have been in vain. Just how worthwhile will never be known, for our Master Himself has said that kindnesses shown to the poor and the suffering are kindnesses shown to Him.

THE TWINS

The date was 1959; the place, the Kwong Wah Charity Hospital, Hong Kong.

The father didn't want the just-born girl twins. Had they been boys he would have wanted them, for he was Chinese and Chinese rate boys higher than girls.

The mother may have wanted them, but she couldn't want them, for there was not room enough and food enough for two more in this family of refugees from Red China in their cubbyhole home.

And so the Chinese mother left her babies to the mercy of the charity hospital where they were born, and returned to her hovel home. "I want that American lady to have them," she said.

"That American Lady" the mother referred to was a relief worker who had been handing out gifts of food and clothing to the average 63 refugee and fisherfolk mothers leaving the hospital daily. (Kwong Wah had the largest maternity ward of any hospital in the world!) At this request of the mother and the insistence of the nurses, That American Lady took the unwanted wee things and named them Faith and Hope. And Nancy Lam Ho, her helper in the distributions, and she went out to find a place for two more in that most densely populated spot on the earth called Hong Kong.

For two weeks the fate of Faith and Hope lay in the balance while That American Lady and Nancy tramped the streets in their behalf trying to find a substitute mother, a baby's home or an orphanage. There were legal matters, too. Like another Baby two thousand years ago for whom there was no room in the inn, there seemed to be no room in all Hong Kong for The Twins. The searchers came near to giving up faith and hope that they would ever find a home for Faith and Hope.

Then one day Nancy said to her mother, "Mother, why don't *we* take the twins?"

The family of Mrs. Kwok Kwan Ho -- Nancy and her brothers Tom and Mark -- were already knee-deep in responsibilities in operating a private school for over one hundred refugee and fisherfolk children, most of whom could pay little or no tuition. How could Mrs. Ho take on an additional responsibility that would demand her day and night attention and put an additional strain on the family finances? But big-hearted people go beyond limits, and Faith and Hope became members of the Ho family.

Although not legally adopted, the babies received love and attention as though they had been. The relief organization which That American Lady represented gave occasional material aid distributions to the Kwok Kwan Day School students, and Professor Tse Johnson, principal of the school, whose wife and son were still in Red China, took a vicarious interest in the twins and helped to ease the load for Mrs. Ho.

Six months later That American Lady returned to America, and occasional letters followed, telling how Faith and Hope were growing from infancy to childhood. Between the lines of some of these letters one could read of financial strain, and then years later came a frank confession of urgent need of help. That American Lady confided the circumstances to a neighbor family, and for some years now that family has been sending its concern for The Twins on the wings of monthly checks.

Time passed and The Twins grew.

Time passed and That American Lady was once again in Hong Kong.

And Sunday morning, January the twenty-fourth, 1971, found Faith and Hope, now eleven years old, smiling and neatly dressed, sitting by the side of That American Lady in the New Life Temple in Hong Kong and listening to a bilingual sermon on "Living Faith," by Evangelist Al Smith of San Diego, California. Professor Johnson had brought The Twins. And Nancy was there, too. It was a time for joy. And how appropriate the sermon subject! Faith and Hope were living because of the living faith and hope that works for those who cared.

But the story is not yet ended.

The family in America had sent word that they would educate the girls in America if That American Lady would bring The Twins back with her. Magnanimously, the Ho family agreed to break affectionate ties and let them go. They felt, however, that The Twins should have one more year in their Chinese school in Hong Kong.

And so the future continues to hold promise for Faith and Hope Ho Lam.

And this story of The Twins is one reason why That American Lady, my wife, made the six-weeks trip to the Orient in the first months of 1971.

Update: The husband of the family intending to bring Faith and Hope to the United States for education, has meanwhile passed away. Nancy

Lam Ho, who had persuaded her mother to adopt The Twins, has also meanwhile met with a harrowing fate: her dismembered body was found on the beach of Hong Kong Harbor. According to latest information, no one has been apprehended of the grisly crime. Faith and Hope feel that they, in turn, should help to take care of Nancy's two young boys. Faith has successfully passed the entrance examination to Hong Kong University, and Hope is completing a business course. They still correspond with That American Lady. Faith writes she has had unusual opportunity for Christian witness in the university.

In all things I have shown you that by so toiling one must help the weak, remembering the words of the Lord Jesus, how He said, 'It is more blessed to give than to receive.'

-The Apostle Paul in Acts 20:35, Revised Version-

MOON PERSPECTIVE

Probably the prize of all pictures which cameras have taken is that of the earth-rise from the moon's surface, shown in TIME's 1973 New Year's issue, and later used on a United States postage stamp.

There she is, our earth, in all her orbital glory, silhouetted against the blackness of space. What perspective this man-achieved view of the earth gives us! The entire home of man defined within the limits of a single photo frame! Grandfather, should you rise from your grave, you'd not believe it!

This is the earth that God created. It is the earth that once wasn't. "Before the world began," the Revelator John says, Christ was sharing the glories of the Father far out there among the galaxies.

It is the earth that Lucifer, the usurper, spoiled when God cast him out of His presence. The earth became chaos.

It is the earth that God re-made into a paradise for man, and promptly Satan caused man to fall, and again spoiled the earth.

It is the earth that since then has become a battleground for Satan against God, with man in the middle.

It is the earth that God's Son came down to to redeem mankind, and it is the earth He returned from to His Father's Throne far out there in space.

And there it is! the entire sphere! on a man-made photograph!

As one holds the earth between finger and thumb, one's imagination is exhausted in trying to fathom the sum of the woe and sin and suffering and troubles that Satan and his cohorts have spread around the surface of the beautiful bright ball, for does not the planet earth "lay in the lap of the Evil One" and is Satan not the "Prince of the Power of the Air?" What a fusion of groans must go up to God from the earth we're looking at!

To assist our feeble imagination toward comprehension of this weight of woe, let's leave our moon perch and get back down to earth, softlanding on a tiny dot just 1/5600th of the earth's total surface.

We find ourselves in Burundi, Africa.

To see the people living on this sliver of land (about the size of New Jersey), we sit without let-up eight days and nights on the reviewing stand as they march past us ten abreast at the rate of two hundred a minute. And each one is a person, a human being who has to cope with hunger, malnutrition, illiteracy, superstition and an annual income of less than one hundred dollars a year. And each hurts and hopes and despairs and loves and hates like you and I!

Multiply each Burundian's woes two and a half million times and try to sense the sorrows and sufferings on just this tiny 1/1120th of Africa's land mass!

Take now the moon-scope photo between finger and thumb again. Can you grasp it? Can you feel the weight of woe and hear the groans that are emanating from the beautiful earth-ball as it hangs out there against the blackness of space?

All these worldly things, these evil desires--the craze for sex, the ambition to buy everything that appeals to you, and the pride that comes from wealth and importance--these are not from God. They are from this evil world itself. And this world is fading away, and these evil, forbidden things will go with it, but whoever keeps doing the will of God will live forever.

-I John 2:16, 17; The Living Bible-

EASTERN GATES

One of my tasks in Japan was to help MCC workers enroute to Korea with getting their military permits for entrance to Korea at the American Occupation Forces Headquarters in Tokyo. Sometimes this took only a few days; at other times, weeks. During this waiting time, the workers lived with us at our Tokyo Center, so that Eunice and I became well acquainted with dozens of MCC workers before they left for their respective fields of service in Korea.

At that time most of the MCCers came to Yokohama by ship. It was a thrill to meet them at the docks and welcome them to Japan, and then, after proper documentation, to wave them farewell as they left by ship or by plane for Seoul or Pusan, Korea.

Katherine Dyck, a registered nurse from Rosthern, Saskatchewan, Canada, was one of these. She arrived at Yokohama in November, 1953, and had considerable difficulty in getting her military permit by reason of her Canadian birth. After some weeks her papers did come through, and we waved her Godspeed as she left for her assigned service at a mothers' clinic in Pusan, Korea.

Katherine's three-year term of service was almost up when one day I received a telegram from Pusan saying that her ice-packed body was being flown to Tokyo; would I please see to its embalming for further shipment to Canada. On August 2, 1956, Katherine and another nurse, Bertha Cornelson, while sitting together by the seaside, had suddenly been swept into churning waters by a tidal wave, and all rescue attempts had proved futile.

And for the second time I met Katherine Dyck at Yokohama. After the embalming, the remains were airlifted to Canada. Bertha Cornelson was buried in Korea.

I have commemorated this event by the following poem, entitled "Eastern Gates." With two other MCC workers, Katherine had originally come through Japan, the "Gateway to the East," but when she left Korea, she went directly to Heaven's "Eastern Gate."

("Chosen," in the poem, is another name for Korea. The accent is on the second syllable.)

Across Pacific's blue once came
Three young goodwill invaders,
Steering a course to Chosen Land --

Three Christian youth crusaders!

The ship rode light, for hearts were light;
In fact, the joy increased
The nearer that the ship did come
To th' "Gateway to the East."

First hove in sight the snow-capped hood
Of high famed Fujiyama,
And then the ship pulled up 'longside
The dock in Yokohama.

I saw it come. I boarded ship.
I grasped the hand of each
And thought I sensed in them a thrill
That's not conveyed by speech.

They lingered just until they got
Their legalized permission
To journey on and carry out
Their MCC commission.

And so in spite of hindrance
'Twas with the one idea
Of serving God and man they spent
Three years in South Korea.

And now with tasks accomplished well
They are returning home;
Already one has said farewell
By Chosen's ocean foam.

I met her yesterday again
At self-same Yokohama.
We did not speak; our meeting was
A sad and silent drama.

Did I say "sad"? Too, I was glad,
For on that bed of chrome
Did lay just lump of clay --
She was already Home!

Although Miss Dyck has lived just half
The years that I have seen,
She finished first her task; her ship
First reached the Heavenly Scene.

I think that when I too at last
Life's voyage terminate,
In turn, *she'll* greet *me* at the dock --
At Heaven's "Eastern Gate!"

DIVORCE NOT CONTEMPLATED

It is a vexing situation to have one's wife sharing her love with others -- to see her discontinuing many housekeeping amenities just to spend more time with her new-found loves -- to find her correspondents wearing items of clothing which she has made away with from her husband's wardrobe.

It is vexing. But such is the lot of a relief-worker husband whose teammate wife lets her boundless sympathies go out to the suffering underprivileged peoples whom they had crossed the seas to help.

My wife has the gift of identification, of putting herself in the place of others. We have served together in relief work in Austria, Japan, Hong Kong and central Africa. Whenever we are settled in a new location, she finds the neediest of the needy, the outcast, the underdog, and in no time at all she is rejoicing with those who rejoice and weeping with those who weep. She writes no articles on economics, but she protests the inequalities which she sees so much of and has a conscience about big dinners, vacations and pleasure spending.

In Africa, it all started with cups of cold water given to head-laden tribespeople as they passed our house to their homes in the hills. Then it was cups of coffee to some of the older women and mothers with children astride their backs as they ventured in from the road to our kitchen door. Soon they were inside the house for rolls and coffee and devotions. And when they were convinced that they had found a friend, they began to confide their troubles.

"Where," asked one of the women of the group one day, "can we find a white woman who just puts you in her house, gives you coffee in her cups, and puts you in her good chairs without worrying? Some of us do not know how to use her cups." And then the speaker added, "It is because she loves us and believes that we have the same Heavenly Father, and that Jesus Christ paid everything so that we might all be equal. We must all love and not hate one another."

Word got around in the Belge, Usumbura's poorest sections, and soon a flock of non-descript unfortunates were trooping the three miles and more up the mountainside for the Sunday service and for the weekday sewing classes she had started. And when they returned to their mud shacks and windowless grass huts, they left behind them sad and tragic stories as well as traces of lower forms of animal life which would have colonized our house had we not used DDT. But my wife was more concerned about the stories than about the bedbugs and lice.

Morning, noon and night this "apostle to the poor" is voluble with schemes and plans for the widows, the homeless, the halt, the lame and the blind whom she has taken under her wing. Almost daily there is a procession of ragged humanity to our door and it breaks her heart to have to turn any away. In a recent clothing distribution two hundred of them turned up for the sixty bundles she had prepared. Sobbing openly as she faced the crowd, she apologized, "I know how much you need these things, but there isn't nearly enough to go around."

It is these bottom-of-the-ladder Africans who have become the contenders for my wife's attention and affection. Her husband, however, is not jealous. He knows there is no dilution in the quality of her love for him. If there has been a run on the bread box during the day, can he complain when she gives him the one slice that's left and she takes the heel? If she gives away his shirt, does he not remember that she once came home from their clothing distribution center without shoes because there were none to fit a refugee woman? He is sometimes vexed, but not perplexed, for he knows that if he gets the short end, she takes the shortest.

There are times when vexation *can* approach perplexity. The role of my wife's husband in the relief team is more prosaic and impersonal than is hers. He arranges for the transportation of hundreds of tons of United States government surplus foods over the rough and mountainous roads of Burundi to two dozen Protestant mission stations for their school and hospital feeding programs. He plans for the distribution of hundreds of bales of clothing donated by Christians in the United States to the 21,000 refugees in three large resettlement camps in eastern Burundi. He brings in large shipments of drugs sent by Christian medical societies in America for Burundi hospitals. There are committee meetings and reports and bookkeeping and interviews and broken-down cars and not enough hours in a day.

Now when two over-full schedules are compressed within the compass of a husband-wife relationship, a great amount of grace is needed from the Lord, especially if each feels deeply a sense of mission. A shipment is being lifted at the port. But a refugee widow and her children have been ejected from their hut and the widow is sick and the car is needed to take her to the hospital. The transfer of the shipment of beans *must* be completed today to avoid a storage charge, says the husband; the woman may die and we *must* get her now, says the wife; and the human appeal wins over the money appeal.

God does give grace. There are perplexities aplenty, but after the day's vexations comes the night's refreshment. In the morning husband and wife look across the table and smile and know that their aims are the same. And during devotions they somehow know that their love for one another and for God is growing stronger in the measure that it flows out to fellow men.

And so in spite of competing loves and competing programs, the relief team carries on. The husband has never contemplated divorce.

Help carry one another's burdens, and in this way you will obey the law of Christ. Let us not become tired of doing good; for if we do not give up, the time will come when we will reap the harvest. So then, as often as we have the chance, we should do good to everyone, and especially to those who belong to our family in the faith.

-Galatians 6:2, 9, 10; The Good News Bible-

THE SHOELESS SHOEMAKER

He had no parents, no wife, no children, no friends, no home, no job, no money, no legs!

He slept on the steps in front of the main gate at Ueno Zoo.

There is one thing he was thankful for; it was that he had no legs for passersby to tramp on in front of the main gate at Ueno Zoo.

He used to be a shoemaker. An accident left him without legs. Then he came from Rubenshibe in Hokkaido to Tokyo. But there was no demand for legless shoemakers in Tokyo, and he gravitated to the bottom job of ragpicking. Hobbling around on his leg-stubs, he scavenged for bits of rags and paper in Tokyo streets and parks, and, as we have just said, slept on the steps in front of the main gate at the Ueno Zoo.

Not long ago he was sick. It was during this sickness he had a dream. Rather, it was a vision, for he saw Christ, beautiful and kind. And the vision did something to him. It made him well and pepped him up and gave him hope.

About that time a foreign lady and some young people came to give a cup of milk to each of two hundred homeless men, women and children who, like he, slept on the steps in front of the main gate at Ueno Zoo. They also sang and prayed and read some words from a book with bright covers.

The music and their kind words struck the responsive chord in his newfound joy, and when these people came back again, and then again, he told them about his happiness. The happiness could be seen. How he whirled about on his short crutches!

Now since this group kept coming every evening, giving out sometimes milk, sometimes solid foods, he got to looking forward to the milk and songs and the kind words as his day's highpoint. "This is the place where my soul belongs," he said, "for it is a great help to come here and pray and sing together with you; it is so refreshing!"

Two weeks after receiving a Book, he reported his progress. "I've read it halfway through," he said proudly. "There are many things I do not understand, but I start reading it at five in the morning, and there is something about it that heartens me to bear the day's burden. As I go about the city gathering rags and waste paper, I think about what I've read in the morning. It is a great pleasure for me."

The foreign lady suddenly recalled at breakfast one morning that she had a complete shoemaker's outfit in her warehouse -- hammers, lasts, and a good supply of leather. For several years she had wondered to whom she might give this equipment. Now she knew. It was as though God had been holding it in reserve for this moment.

Next day the Shoeless Shoemaker set up his shoe repair shop. It was just a little booth on the sidewalk. He called it "The Shop of Hope," and now when his customers wait while he repairs their shoes, he tells them what God has done, his radiant face adding weight to his testimony.

And now came other big news; he had found a life companion, and would it be possible for them to have a Christian wedding?

The foreign lady thought maybe so. Her husband would soon be back from a long journey, and then maybe he would perform the ceremony.

And when the husband consented, the Shoeless Shoemaker pounded more vigorously at his last and joined still more lustily in the evensongs on the steps in front of the main gate at Ueno Zoo.

The group of Japanese young people and the foreign lady prepared the veil and baked five layer-cakes so that everyone of the 200 ragpicker's buddies could have a piece.

And six days ago, as this story is being written,* there was an open-air Christian wedding in this, Tokyo's most notorious slum area, and the happy little man beside the smiling bride was the Shoeless Shoemaker. The foreign lady brought and handed out the cake and orange punch; the husband, who just one month previously had been ordained to the ministry, performed the ceremony, the group of young Japanese sang appropriate songs, and the ragpicker's pals filed past the happy pair to offer congratulations. One of the metropolitan newspapers headlined the pictured story, "The Blue-Sky Wedding."

"I'm a newborn man," the groom said to four cars of reporters at the wedding. "We have both quit drinking and smoking, and want to live as sincere Christians." There was no mistaking he meant it. And the earnestness was reflected the following day in the undistorted, respectful stories carried in Tokyo's three largest newspapers.

Thus with a single bound, the erstwhile homeless, jobless, friendless, hopeless, ragpicking Shoeless Shoemaker projected a sincere Christian witness of his transformed life to the millions of avid newspaper readers in all Japan, a witness more telling than many a cloistered sermon!

The foreign lady and the Japanese young people still give the cups of milk, and read the bright-backed Book, but the Shoeless Shoemaker and his bride say they are looking for a place where they can establish a home and live as normal people. They have left their old haunts on the steps in front of the main gate at Ueno Zoo!

(Note: Ueno is a downtown park in Tokyo. Before the War it had been a cultural center, with art and science museums and zoo. But during the War it deteriorated to a black marketeer's mart. It is still, ten years after the War, the gathering place of racketeers, white slavers, bootleggers, and human derelicts of a society that has not yet fully recovered from the shock of the War. Two hundred ragpickers and nondescript sleep here in the open. It is to these that MCC serves milk every evening, and follows up with songs and a short message. We are grateful for this special privilege which the metropolitan police have given us. NAW.)

Do not store up riches for yourselves here on earth, where moths and rust destroy, and robbers break in and steal. Instead, store up riches for yourselves in heaven, where moths and rust cannot destroy, and robbers cannot break in and steal. For your heart will always be where your riches are.

-Matthew 6:19-21, The Good News Bible-

---

* (October 30, 1955)

JOEY AND JIMMY
A Tale of Two Brothers

I can see him yet as his mother brought him piggyback up the seventy-six stairsteps to our Mennonite Central Committee Relief Center in Hong Kong. We wondered, I remember, why this woman with the sore and swollen legs should be toting her five-and-a-half-year-old so pamperingly. Inescapable of our notice, too, was a startling contrast between mother and son. Whereas the face of the mother was pure Chinese, that of the son showed European characteristics. The incrustation of dirt that surely must have been an accumulation of weeks could not conceal the difference. Indeed, were the boy to be seen in a London or Reedley street setting, no one would suspect that there was Chinese blood in his veins. Yet he spoke -- when he spoke -- Chinese, and Chinese only.

Two days earlier the mother came to us for the first time, this human being without a permanent abode. The grimy face and feet, the disheveled hair, and the dirty dress screamed more loudly for help than did the woman's feeble request. The big Hong Kong fire of 1953, as we were to learn later, had left this once happily and wealthily married woman husbandless and homeless, and was the beginning of the toboggan slide that landed her finally among the street sleepers of Kowloon, Hong Kong. Whether it was due to the bit of halting English which she spoke, or to the confusion of a mental imbalance, I do not know, but one got the impression that the little information she gave was but a trickle of the dammed-up pool of unrevealed misery. What a figure! There she stood, a classic end product of Satanic wiles and furies!

Did we talk to her about the love of God? Did we say to her, "Go, be fed and clothed. God bless you?" No! We could not! Instead, we soaped and soaked and scrubbed and lysoled and reclothed, and hoped at the same time that there might be a softening of the grime incrustation of heart and soul as well. Then we gave her additional clothing for herself and for the two boys she said she had: one five-and-a-half and the other eight, both of whom were also floating around somewhere on Kowloon streets.

A missionary friend who was at the center at the time accompanied the woman as the latter led her in a deviously roundabout way to her "home" which proved to be a narrow open space between two buildings. We did not see her again until she appeared at our center with the mixed-blood, dirty-faced, five-and-a-half-year-old urchin.

It was a case of love at first sight. There was an indescribable quality of innocence and passiveness about the lad that made him crawl right into one's heart. As an expression of our "first love," we had the boy crawl right into the bathtub and gave him the works the same as his mother had received two days before, plus a thorough delousing of his sandy hair.

A second expression of our concern was a swift decision, agreed to by the mother, that the boy remain at the center. It would certainly have been inhuman on our part to permit this child, who still had his baby teeth, to return to his old life of begging and pickpocketing and of finding food and sleep by chance on Kowloon streets. It should be understood that although it was likely mother love that prompted the woman to bring her boy to the center, usually mother and son each went his homeless way, for the life of the beggar and the prostitute, whether young or old, normally causes the flame of human affection to burn low, and each must fend for himself.

We called our little guest "Joey."

Joey adapted himself quickly to his new environment. Although the details of his tender years still remain unclear, all indications were that this was the child's first experience of normal family life. And he liked it. He was finding something here he had not known much of before, for street urchins get little true affection from the passing throng. Once when my wife lay down beside him, Joey, the child, put his arms tenderly around her neck and fell asleep.

That was the child Joey. But there was also the worldly-wise adult Joey. Emphatically, we have never seen such an old five-and-a-half-year-old child. Life's rugged experience had sharpened both wits and wisdom in the art of survival. It had brought out in him, the Eurasian, the cunning of the Oriental and the aggressiveness of the Occidental. The "innocence and passiveness" shown when he first came to the center on his mother's back were not due to shyness, not by a long way. Joey had learned to use his childhood wiles to good advantage.In begging, the innocence and the captivating smile paid off, and in pickpocketing, they softened the consequences when he was caught.

I have seen the court record of Joey's arrest by the police for panhandling in the Star Ferry Arcade. Across the bottom of the record was written, "Too young to charge." He was let off with a warning and a gift of five dollars by the court. Several times in his off-guard moments, Joey would demonstrate to us the technique of pickpocketing. He would hold up his left hand for an alms as he walked by the side of the tourist stranger, and at the same time reach into the pocket with his right hand, drop the money to the pavement, walk a few steps farther, and then return to pick up the money.

This doubleness in Joey's character became more evident the longer he was with us. Every nerve in him was on its toes. He was observant and resourceful. When he was hurt, he wouldn't cry. His actions betrayed that his street games had been fighting and gambling. Yet as days passed, he let down his guard more and more and revealed himself for the child he really was: loving, lovable and surprisingly unselfish. On his own initiative one day, he crawled up on the kitchen table, poured a glass of hot water from the thermos, put in several teaspoons of sugar, and carried it to my wife who was in bed with a cold.

I shall always remember the time when Joey and I went to the YMCA for ice cream. As we walked hand in hand, memory's clock clicked back the years, and the little hand in mine became that of our own Sonny Boy. Joey let me see into his child-heart that day, and what I saw there was sincere and unstaged. The smiles and the sidlings-up were the child's responses to a paternal love it had not known before. Incidents such as this were threads which the days were twisting into cords, cords that were going to be hard to break.

In the hallway entrance to our building is a curio and gift shop. Among the items for sale there are Chinese puzzles. They are complicated things, made out of two pieces of wire bent into dozens of curves and angles. They resemble illustrations of mazes in psychology textbooks. With only a hammer, a pair of pliers, and a two-inch-square iron block, a former Shanghaiese sits all day in the narrow shop, bending straight pieces of wire into these amazing shapes. We came to call him "the puzzle man."

This puzzle man and his wife had been neighbors to Joey's mother back there when she was still living happily with her well-to-do Chinese husband, and now that the hapless woman had become driftwood on Kowloon streets, the continued concern of her neighbors prompted them to ask MCC to help her with food and clothing. It was the puzzle man who looked for and found and brought the woman to our relief center. And the woman, as the reader knows, brought Joey.

But where was the woman's older child, the one born in happy wedlock?

Joey said he knew.

So after some days at the center, Joey and the puzzle man set out to find the older Chinese brother.

Did Joey lead the puzzle man to a school to find his brother? Yes, he did. He led him to a first-class school, one of the most up-to-date schools of crime in the Far East. He led him into that patch of shacks and winding lanes which is known as "Inner Kowloon," or the "Walled City," where there is no law, no police, and where the "schoolrooms" are heroin and opium dens and prostitution houses, and the "laboratories," hiding places where crimes are hatched. Even the puzzle man was puzzled that the boy knew his way so well on the campus of this graduate school of human dereliction.

Joey found the place, but not his brother. The place was a space under a bed, the occupant of which, a mother who had taken pity on the homeless boy, permitted him to sleep there nights. The day before the visit of Joey and the puzzle man, the boy had broken a bowl and did not return to his accustomed place that night for fear of reprisals by the manager of the place. The puzzle man paid for the broken bowl, hoping that the boy would return again to his under-the-bed bed. The search mission was thus a failure.

But the puzzle man continued his concern. Thinking he could find the place again without Joey's guidance, he set out very early one morning several days later to look for the boy. But the narrow winding lanes within that crooked inner city were like his own puzzles' mazes, and he got lost. An inquiry for direction revealed that he was not a denizen of the place, and he had to pay some bribes to be permitted to proceed. At last he found the place -- and the boy!

The reader must here understand the danger that attended the puzzle man's rescue mission. The eight-year-old was a shoeshine boy. His earnings ranged from two to four Hong Kong dollars a day, all of which -- except thirty cents -- he had to hand over to criminal elements as "protection" money. This gave him the "privilege" of an assigned street where there would be no competition. The boy was, literally, a slave; and it is not hard to understand what a financial loss the boy's disappearance would entail and what lengths might be employed to circumvent his leaving. But it was early morning, and the mission was negotiated safely.

A little later that same day the half-brothers were reunited.

We called the new arrival "Jimmy."

Like Joey and his mother, Jimmy, too, now got the works: bathtub, soap, lysol, haircut. Although Jimmy was nearly three years older than Joey, he stood only slightly taller, and his malnutritioned body weighed less than did his brother's. We outfitted Jimmy from an MCC bale of boys' clothing. A junior sailor's suit fit him so snugly it must have been intended for him.

On the calf of one of Jimmy's toothpick legs were teeth scars where someone had bitten deep into the flesh. The story is too tragic to tell. The wound had been infected, but now was healed over.

The first hours of the boys' reunion was like the casual throws in the warming-up period before a baseball game. There was restraint and a sizing-up of the situation. Being an old resident at the center, Joey showed Jimmy the ropes. The boys soon made themselves at home. The game was started, and from then on there was never a dull moment.

The doubleness of character, previously mentioned regarding Joey, became still more evident now that the boys were together. At one moment they would act like the children they were, interested in everything and responsive to our every suggestion. At the next moment, they would revert to their street characters, enjoy a fist fight, and fill the air -- so we were told -- with gutter words and underworld shop talk. They were a junior version of Dr. Jekyll and Mr. Hyde.

As the days went by the boys reverted less and less frequently to the street roles. They did not care to go out of the house. They evidenced no desire to return to their old ways of living. As was to be expected, they were sometimes rude, and often exceedingly tricky, but we can truthfully say they were not really bad. Joey delighted to use his sleight of hand to make things disappear, but to our knowledge he never stole from us. He would lock a door and hide the key, have a hearty laugh while we stewed over the matter, and then give back the key. One day while he accompanied my wife in her hospital distributions, he showed her her own watch on his wrist. He had picked it up that morning from her dresser.

Both boys ate like woodchoppers. Undoubtedly they had never enjoyed such a varied fare. It was a delight to see them seated at our table with bowls to mouth, shoving rice, Chinese fashion, into the cavernous stomachs.

Never did our shoes get such frequent shinings. It was the one way by which they could say thank you. Both boys could twist the daubing rag and crack the shine cloth the professional way. They used a can of condensed milk powder for a footstool.

Early evening found J and J going strong. It wasn't until late that they were finally run down. Sometimes we would coax them to bed too early, and then pay the price of a sleepless hour of jabber and laughter and a half dozen excuse-trips to the toilet. But when we would at last look down on the homeless lads as they lay fast asleep in the floor bed by the side of our own, our thoughts would start spinning more of those threads that were fast being twisted into heart-binding cords.

In spite of the growing attachment, however, we well knew that the boys weren't ours, and that a course of action would have to be decided soon. We were also not unaware of the seriousness of our moves, for decisions having to do with human beings, like railroad switches, determine destinies.

One thing we were sure of: The boys must not go back to the streets.

If only it were possible for the half-brothers to go together to Children's Garden, the million-dollar orphanage in the New Territories opened last summer by the Christian Children's Fund Organization! Improbable, we thought, but worth trying.

Happily, the answer was favorable. They would be glad to take the lads, they said, providing the case be cleared first through the Hong Kong government's Social Welfare Office. If the boys could be taken into the government's receiving home until the legal points were resolved, then transfer to the Children's Garden would be possible.

But what about the mother during the weeks her boys were with us?

After she had lugged Joey up the six flights of stairsteps, she kept returning frequently to the center. In fact, her oft-coming was a bit aggravating. Not that we had no sympathy for her, but all our efforts to help her seemed so frustrated. Whether the apparent irresponsibility was due to willfulness on her part, or to mental illness, we do not know. Money we gave her for finding shelter, for example, apparently went for nonessentials. Finally we personally accompanied her for an interview with the relieving officer of Yaumate Kaifong Center who issued her a card for one hot meal a day, and found night shelter for her in one of the quonset huts of the Street Sleepers Shelter Society.

Joey usually had little to do with his mother when she called at our center. Again, on the day Jimmy came, there was not the joyous mother-son reunion one would naturally expect under the situation. In truth, it is a sad thing to have to report that neither of the boys showed any marked degree of respect for their mother. Whose fault it was, who can say? The leg scar may be at least a partial answer.

Nonetheless, the woman was the boys' mother, and, as such, needed to be consulted regarding their future. Explaining to her that our work as a relief organization made it impossible for us to keep them longer, we urged that she agree to the above-mentioned plans. Her former neighbor, the puzzle man, also strongly recommended the proposed course of action. The mother finally gave her consent.

We did not tell Joey and Jimmy about the change until the day they were to leave. They had become suspicious of any move that might rob them of the affection and food and fun that they had found in the new "Utopia." They had had a taste of decent, normal living, and they liked it and were on guard against any decoy that might lead them back into their old life.

Then, when the visitors from Social Welfare came for the boys, it did not take long for the sharp-witted lads to sense there was something in the air. Jimmy crawled under the bed. Joey trickily hid in corners and behind doors. Their thoughts were on what they were leaving, and not on what they were going to, in spite of the glowing prospects held out to them. It took some fast thinking and long persuading to get the boys to go, even reluctantly, with their benefactors. But the resistance evaporated quickly, and when we visited the receiving home two days later we found the boys in their usual bubbling spirits.

The story of Joey and Jimmy now comes to a quick and happy ending.

Within two weeks after they had given us our last shoeshine and had eaten their last breakfast at our table, they found themselves at Children's Garden, thanks to the fine cooperation of Government Welfare and Christian Children's Fund. We had not really expected that our dream for them would so soon come true.

Two weeks later still, we visited our boys at Children's Garden. They were their enthusiastic selves. They led us to their cottage home, introduced us to their housemother, showed us where they were going to school. "We have morning worship here just like we did at Grandpa's house," Jimmy said reminiscingly. Like colts just let out of stable and frisking in open field, the onetime grime-encrusted ragamuffins were plainly enjoying their new life in the fresh air of this idyllic spot.

But Joey and Jimmy were no longer *our boys*. They had found a good mother and brothers and sisters and were well-adjusted and happy. And we would not have had it otherwise.

Strange, though, how strong a cord those threads made in so short a time!

TRIBES IN RWANDA AND BURUNDI

Anthropologists have placed the Twa Pygmies as the earliest inhabitants of this heart-of-Africa tableland. With the dawning of recorded history, the Hutus, a race of peaceful agriculturalists of Bantu origin, had supplanted the Pygmies and taken over most of the land.

Then about 400 years ago, the Tutsis, a tall pastoral tribe of Hamitic origin, began a mass migration from Ethiopia and gradually infiltrated the Hutu tribespeople. In their thousand-mile trek from the northeast, the Tutsis brought with them their all-important lyre-horned cattle, important not so much as a source of food, as a status symbol; the more cattle a man owned, the higher he rated in the tribal social scale. Also the cow became the basis of the so-called "client system," a device for inter-tribal cooperation, the abuse of which was eventually to explode in a series of violent coups.

The gradual subjection of the majority Hutus by the Tutsi newcomers was on this wise:

As the food producers, the Hutus, at the start, had had control of the land in Rwanda and Burundi. With the arrival of the Tutsis, there gradually evolved between the two tribes a system of mutual exchange. Initially, it was land for cattle. Gradually, the Tutsis maneuvered things so that when the Hutus desired more cattle they received them in exchange for working the land for the Tutsis. Eventually, the cattle were not even given to the Hutus as total property, but only to be used for milk-giving.

When one questions why the Hutus allowed themselves to be thus dominated by the Tutsis, one must bear in mind that the Tutsis were warriors whom the Hutus looked upon as their protectors. They were undoubtedly willing to give much to the Tutsis for the security which allowed them to pursue in peace their life of cultivation. Thus, it seemed to be a natural evolution which allowed the Tutsis to secure a superior position and influence. The Tutsis began to enjoy all the privileges. They also could put some pressure on the Hutus to oblige them with goods and services. The culture and traditions of each tribe also helped to define their relationship. For the Hutus, there was nothing to hold them together. Authority was based on ability. They used army and government as testing grounds for their ability.

Thus, over the intervening centuries, the fine-featured, aristocratic invaders gradually reduced the passive, hard-working Hutus to the status of serfs. Although there were spotty disagreements and minor revolts, by and large, the Hutu peasantry accepted almost fatalistically their subservient role in the central African society; that's just the way things were! But by the middle of the twentieth century there was building up within them resentment against their tall, autocratic masters. And with the winds of freedom and independence now blowing across Africa, they became more keenly aware of their serfdom and wondered why they, who outnumbered their overlords more than five to one, should be their slaves.

The friction between the Hutu and the Tutsi tribespeople increased through the 1960's and 1970's. There were rebellions by the Hutus, followed by counter-coups by the Tutsi, climaxing in the bloodbath perpetrated by the Tutsi.

- *No Place to Stop Killing* - pp. 23, 24

Where do all the fights and quarrels among you come from? They come from your desires for pleasure, which are constantly fighting within you. You want things, but you cannot have them, so you are ready to kill; you strongly desire things, but you cannot get them, so you quarrel and fight. You do not have what you want because you do not ask God for it. And when you ask, you do not receive it, because your motives are bad; you ask for things to use for your own pleasure.

-James 4:1-3, The Good News Bible-

TWO CHRISTIAN MARTYRS
One Was a Tutsi Tribesman

There were Tutsi tribesmen in Rwanda whose homes had been destroyed in the initial rebellion of 1959 and 1961 but who did not leave the country. These were called "displaced persons," and were resettled in an area in southern Rwanda, called Nyamata. Like Tutsi refugee camps outside Rwanda, this displaced persons camp needed to be provided for, and a great deal of our MCC material aid was sent to Nyamata.

An outstanding Christian leader who was shepherding the Christians in Nyamata developed a network of 24 village churches, organized around a mother church, to serve 6,000 people. He was also responsible for the out-schools with their 26 primary teachers. This very devoted Christian leader was Bishop Yono Kanamuzeyi. During the reign of terror in the Nyamata area at the end of 1963, Brother Yono knew that his time was coming and that his days were numbered.

And so it was! The following impressive and thrilling story was related by a fellow Christian, Andrew Kayumba, who himself was miraculously spared:

"On Thursday, January 23, 1964, at seven o'clock in the evening, a Jeep with five soldiers in the command of the senior sergeant arrived in front of Pastor Kanamuzeyi's house. They called to him to come outside. He went immediately with a stout heart, trusting God.

"Two of the soldiers came to my house and told me that I was wanted. When I went outside I found my friend Yono already there. They told me to climb into the Jeep; they would take us to the lieutenant. So off we went to the military camp at Nyamata.

"When we arrived at the camp, they took us into a room where we found another man sitting on the floor. After a time the soldiers returned without the lieutenant and told us to climb into the Jeep again, all three of us. The Jeep went down the road toward Kigali (the capital of Rwanda). When Yono saw where we were going, he said to me, 'Let us surrender our lives into God's hands.' He did not say this because of any evil he had done, but because for many days he had seen soldiers doing this very thing with other people and they never returned.

"We went on our way, crossing the River Nyanbarongo, and a little way on the farther side we saw eight more soldiers. They ordered us out of the Jeep. When we got out they told us to surrender everything we had. The third man had a small suitcase which he put on the ground and I put my watch on this case.

"Yono asked for permission to write in his diary. He wrote: 'We are going to heaven,' and then he gave an accounting of the church money left in his house. He placed the diary with the key of his cupboard on the case, as well as also a few francs from his pocket. He asked the senior sergeant to see that his wife be given these things. The sergeant then said, 'You had better pray to your God.'

"We all stood up and Yono prayed: 'Lord, God, You know that we have not sinned against the government, and now I pray You, in Your mercy, accept our lives. And we pray You to avenge our innocent blood, and help these soldiers who do not know what they are doing. In the name of Jesus Christ, our Lord. Amen.'

"Then we were commanded to sit down. They brought ropes and tied our hands behind our backs. One soldier was told to take Yono away, but before they went, we all sang the hymn, 'There is a happy land where saints in glory stand.' And when we had finished singing, they took Yono away.

"And as they went, Yono asked me, 'Do you believe?' And I said, 'Yes, I believe, because we read that whosoever believes will be saved.'

"Then he went, singing:

There's a land that is fairer than day,
And by faith we can see it afar;
For the Father waits over the way,
To prepare us a dwelling place there.

"The soldier took him back to the bridge. There they shot him and threw his body into the water.

"I was left sitting with the other man and the soldiers. They were all amazed. They had never seen anyone go singing to his death, and walking like a man taking a stroll.

"The soldiers called me and I went. They ordered me to sit again and asked if anyone had an axe or a knife. I thought that perhaps they were going to cut me up as they had done many others. They asked me my name and then they returned my watch to me. I asked them to keep it and to send it to my wife, but they ordered me to put it on. They then put me into the Jeep again, and, leaving the third man on the road with some of the soldiers, we returned to the camp. Then they told me to go home, warning me that I had seen the killing of our pastor and that if I said anything about it to anyone, I too would be killed.

"God in His mercy sent a man to lead me through the bush so that I might flee to another country.

"The death of this man of God truly amazed the soldiers who saw him die praying for his enemies.

"I, Andrew Kayumba, whom God has saved from death, write these words and they are true."

Before his death, I once sat in committee meeting with Brother Kanamuzeyi. After the business session, he extended his special thanks for the relief goods we were providing for his people. Then he requested that I pass on his thanks to the Christian people in the States and Canada who have provided funds, food and clothing. This I have done.

Never take revenge, my friends, but instead let God's anger do it. For the scripture says, 'I will take revenge, I will pay back, says the Lord.' Instead, as the scripture says, 'If your enemy is hungry, feed him; if he is thirsty, give him a drink; for by doing this you will make him burn with shame.'

-Romans 12:19, 20; The Good News Bible-

The Other Martyr Was a Hutu Tribesman

The second Christian martyr whose story I share is Abel Binyoni. He was the principal of a mission school during our two years in Burundi. He was also the leader of a local indigenous Friend's Church to which we supplied considerable amounts of food, clothing and medicines for their school and hospital. Before we left Burundi, we received a letter of thanks from Abel for what we did for his church.

"More than anything else," he said, "your gifts teach us the love that is in Jesus Christ which you have shown both for those you've seen and for those you have not seen. It also teaches us that those who help others will be the ones who receive the greatest blessing in their hearts, in their bodies and in their possessions. We pray God that He may bless your gardens, your land, your farm animals, your work, your money, your country and your strength. We bid you farewell in the name of Jesus our Lord."

Brother Binyoni was taken in the bloodbath of 1972. They took him to a place other than his home for execution. No one would have known of the glorious homegoing of this brother in Christ had not a Christian soldier reported back to his friends the details of his death. As they were standing him up to be shot, Brother Abel asked for the privilege of singing, for he was an accomplished musician. His request was granted. He then sang through all four verses of the gospel song, "Jesus, I Come."

Out of my bondage, sorrow, and night, Jesus, I come, Jesus, I come;
Into the glorious gain of Thy cross, Jesus, I come to Thee;
Out of earth's sorrows into Thy balm; out of life's storm and into Thy calm;
Out of distress to jubilant psalm, Jesus, I come to Thee.

Then they shot him.

The soldier reported that there was a pronounced period of hesitation when the order was given to fire. The ringing Christian testimony had had its effect.

And Hutu Martyr Abel Binyoni struck glad hands with Tutsi Martyr Yono Kanamuzeyi in the heavenly home about which both of them sang as they went to their deaths!

AN OPEN DOOR

The Marquis Hosogawa, a titled, multimillionaire Japanese noble, studied for some years before the War at Oxford University. In England, he hobnobbed with earls and lords, and when he returned to Japan he brought back with him not only British culture but also materials to build himself a house after the fashion of the massive British castles. A house of thirty rooms it was, with marbled hallways, spacious staircases and ten bathrooms. Some of the rooms were for tatami, others had inlaid wooden floors. Its location was on a wooded tract near to Waseda University. Date of its erection was 1937.

Came then the War when personal fortunes melted away. No longer could the Marquis maintain his mansion, and so the house stood dark and cold. And one year ago* the house and the spacious ground on which it stood were sold at bargain price.

The purchaser, a Tokyo businessman and multimillionaire, intended to raze the massive pile and in its place raise four other buildings. But the cost of demolition was prohibitive, and so he is building *around* the huge house.

Three large dormitories for students, each housing 200, are now half-built, as is also a student center. By early fall 600 students from two dozen universities in Tokyo will move into the buildings, thus relieving somewhat the critical shortage of rooms for students in Tokyo. The project is non-profit; in fact, it is not even self-sustaining, for rent rates are to be low for the sake of poor students.

The philanthropist, Mr. Kisaku Maekawa, is an idealist, in fact, a very religious man. In another project he had given over a house for the use of all religions, but he has confessed it to be a failure. He now leans strongly toward Christianity. He has given the name "Wakeijuku" to his new dormitory project. Cost of the four buildings is $900,000.

Hearing of MCC through a former classmate's widow who is our neighbor, he sent word for us to come and teach an evening English class to the 50 students already in the old mansion. This we have been doing since October. The Project Manager, in showing us through the building's mazes, asked, "Can you not use these big rooms to some advantage?" We remarked it would be fine for our Open House event. And remembering that we would soon have to move, we hinted the thought of MCC's moving into a few of the empty rooms. This would have been okayed but the fact of our having two girls in our household caused a tabling of the question. MCC did, however, hold its Bible Class Christian Christmas party there. Mr. Maekawa and his son were present. It was his first experience of a Christian Christmas celebration. He was deeply impressed.

Before Christmas he had invited us to a sukiyaki dinner in his home. His gracious wife and kimonoed daughter served us. That evening will always be memorable for the profound words Mr. Maekawa spoke there in the intimacy of his family. "I am a religious man," he said. "I want to be an honest man, but the practices of the business world make me do things I dislike. Money is dirty, money is filthy. I think I should give it all away before I die. God has given me the ability to make money (he manufactures ice and ice boxes). I feel that I must give it back to Him. In fact, actually I do not own anything; everything I have God has given to me: my money, my wife, this house, my body, and (reaching to his head) even the hairs on my head. That is why I am building the dormitories. That is why I expect to sell this house and a factory."

Last week I got word that I was to teach Bible and not English. Mr. Maekawa said to me: "There must be a spiritual atmosphere around this place. Since ten to twenty percent of the 600 students here will be Christian, I am building a chapel in the student center. I want you to live here to make cultural contacts with the students. I am going to build you a house. How many rooms do you need? Do you want the house to be Western style or Japanese style? You can be sure you'll get it; I do not lie."

The words almost took my breath away, and silently I thanked God, for the house will be finished just about the time that MCC will have to move from the present location. I did not teach my class that evening; instead I hurried home to tell my wife and Dr. and Mrs. Melvin Gingerich what God had done. And we have been praying ever since that God might give us grace to live the Christian witness in the midst of these 600 students from the major universities of Tokyo.

Sequel: Mr. Maekawa did keep his word. He built a two-story house on the Wakeijuku campus which he gave us rent-free until our transfer to Hong Kong.

---

* (This article was written March 3, 1957.

AFTER MANY DAYS

For obvious reasons he must remain nameless. He came as a refugee from mainland China to Hong Kong. He was rich and was able to build his wealth into gold bars which he smuggled into free Hong Kong.

In Hong Kong, with all restraints gone, he lived it up. He rented a mansion and lived in grandiose style. He drew to himself a circle of friends, money- and pleasure-lovers like himself. It was wonderful, and it seemed like this fairylike life would never end.

But it did, completely and disastrously! He turned to dope. Dope turned on him. And instead of a mansion, he found himself sleeping on the bare benches of a church, entirely forsaken by his former "friends."

His only friend now was the Christian pastor of the church in which he was sleeping. The pastor was a different kind of friend, one who loved him, not his money; one who with real Christian concern prayed with him and gave himself to help break the dope habit.

Since the Mennonite Central Committee was at that time engaged in a mass feeding program in Hong Kong, the pastor told the head cook about him. The cook who was once a refugee also, had miraculously found Christ at the time he was contemplating suicide. He, in turn, joined with the pastor in an all-out effort to redeem this "hopeless" addict.

Happily, "hopeless" was the wrong word. With the sympathetic and longsuffering concern of the two Christian men and with help from God, he made the slow but complete withdrawal from the habit. To encourage him in his further restoration, the cook invited him to be his helper in the daily MCC feedings, and MCC contributed material aid and spiritual encouragement toward his further rehabilitation.

He had had some medical training in China, and through his Judo training he had become an expert in bone-setting and muscle massage. He was encouraged to open a small office, and this he did.

Eleven years later, in 1971, when Mrs. Wingert was visiting Hong Kong again, he sent word inviting her to a dinner in her honor.

The dinner proved to be a typical Chinese "feast." There were a dozen guests, including the former head cook. Mrs. Wingert learned that in these eleven years he had become a successful doctor in Hong Kong. "We are all, indeed, brothers and sisters in Jesus Christ," he commented at the dinner.

The point of this story is, of course, that "love's labor is never lost." It may take years to see the results of material and spiritual aid given in the name of Christ. Indeed, I am inclined to think that most of the results of mission and relief work remain unrevealed in this present world. Only God knows it all.

God is not unfair. He will not forget the work you did or the love you showed for Him in the help you gave and are still giving to your fellow Christians.
-Hebrews 6:10, The Good News Bible-

IN CHRIST THERE IS NO BLACK OR WHITE

Cosima lives in the heart of Africa
He is coal black
He is tall and straight
His white teeth shine when he smiles

A century and a half ago one of Cosima's forebears had been kidnapped
by slavers--treacherously! cruelly!--and
was sold in the United States

In a grass hut, Cosima's ancestral home, the story
passed down through the generations that
their forefather had been made a slave
to a white man across a big water

Three months ago Cosima came to ask us for work
He did not know we were Americans
He did not know we came from the country where our
white people had made his great great great grandfather
work for them for nothing

We hired Cosima to be our night watchman
He was to guard us and our house from robbers--us, whose people had
robbed *him* of his great great great grandfather

But Cosima is Christian
He did not hold it against us even after he learned who we are
We like Cosima
We think he likes us

We are not "black" and "white"
We are Christian brothers

But there are Africans who know that there were millions
of their people stolen out of their heart-shaped continent
and diamonds
and gold
and other products
and, unlike Cosima, they have not forgiven white men

And now that independence is in the air
many white men are having to leave

Would that the early tradesmen in Africa had all had
the heart of a Livingstone
white men would not be leaving now

In our morning devotions, Cosima
and William our interpreter
and Bitwe our yardman
and we Americans
are hoping and
are praying daily that Christians of all
races may live and work together in love and peace
FOR IN CHRIST THERE IS NO EAST OR WEST, NO WHITE OR BLACK

Do for others what you want them to do for you; this is the meaning of the Law of Moses and of the teachings of the prophets.
-Matthew 7:12, The Good News Bible-

UNDER THE BAMBOO TREES

by William Rukundo

Around 150 very poor Africans come to our Center on a mountainside on Sunday mornings to get a piece of bread and a cup of coffee, and to hear some Bible stories. They start to come at seven o'clock. At a little after nine o'clock they go into the yard and sit on grass mats under the bamboo trees and wait patiently to hear a Bible story

One morning we had an unexpected speaker. It was a big surprise for everyone.

Mrs. Wingert's helper and interpreter, William Rukundo, started the service by singing "Jesu Arankunda," which is Kirundi for "Jesus Loves Me." Everybody seemed to be happy and wanted to keep on singing. William continues the story:

"I read the eighth chapter of John and talked about the blind man who wanted to be healed. When Jesus made him to see, the people would not believe what they saw. They asked the blind man's parents if their son had really been blind. The parents said, 'Our son is of age; he can explain. Ask him.' The son said, 'All I know is that I was blind and that I can really see now.' Then I told my people that everyone is blind in his heart until Jesus gives spiritual sight, but that like the blind man in the story, each one of us must ask for it.

"I then told them another story. There lived one time with an old lady in a village a mother dog and her puppies. The mother dog was very much worried about a hyena that came into the village sometimes. She knew that the hyena wanted to eat her puppies. She told her puppies over and over that whenever they saw the hyena they should run fast and go into the old lady's hut through a hole which the old lady had made for them. The hole was big enough for the puppies, but not for the hyena.

"But the puppies did not obey their mother's advice. One day somebody killed a cow and the whole village ate meat that night. Afterward the puppies gathered up a lot of good bones that were lying around and were just starting to enjoy a real feast when their mother smelled the familiar scent of the hyena.

"Very much excited, the mother called her puppies to follow her quickly to the hole. But some of the puppies kept on eating their nice bones. Others of them followed her quickly to the hole. Others followed their mother and brought their bones with them, but the bones were too big and would not let the puppies get through the hole.

"In no time at all the hyena ate up not only the puppies that were far away from the hole, but also those who were just outside. All of them could have been saved from the hyena if they had left their bones and escaped into the hole. They lost their lives because they did not want to give up the nice bones.

"I said people are like those puppies. People like to have nice sins that they want to enjoy. The Bible warns that if we do not give them up, Satan, our hyena, will destroy us. But like the puppies, we like our pleasant sins too much to give them up.

"There is a way to escape from Satan, for Jesus said, 'I am the Door,' but we cannot take our sin-bones along in with us. We must leave them outside. It is for each of us to decide if we will go through the door and escape from Satan, or will continue in our wicked ways of living and be destroyed. Like the blind man, we must *want* to be healed of the things that are wrong with us.

"When I finished speaking, then came the big surprise. A woman who had never spoken to us before, asked for permission to say a few words.

" 'My fellow women,' she said, 'You must know that when I was young I was blind, like the man in the Bible story we just heard about. And like the puppies, I had many sins. I used to drink. I used to go around with other men. Sometimes I spent a thousand francs in one night in the bars trying to find happiness and peace. But I was never satisfied at all. There was not much meat on the bones. Besides, I did not know that that old hyena, Satan, was trying to catch me.

" 'Then one day not long after my husband died, I was healed of my blindness. I could see Satan coming after me. I dropped my bones and escaped through the Door to where I was safe. I became a Christian. Now I don't go to the bars any more to look for rich men to take me home and give me money. For six years I have been working at the African Hospital washing the dirty bodies of patients when they arrive. I get little, but feel satisfied. I tell you, without Jesus in your heart you cannot feel happy. I have peace in my heart.'

"The unexpected speaker continued in a high voice, 'My fellow women, escape before Satan catches you with all your sins; come quickly to the hole where Satan cannot pass through. You are blind in your heart. Wake up. Leave your drinking and all sorts of things you have in your heart. You cannot get through the gate to Heaven with even one sin-bone in your mouth.

" 'We Africans in Burundi are free now since our independence a year ago, but I ask you here, are you free from your sins? There is no reason for traveling twelve kilometers to hear the wonderful Bible stories and then return to your house not feeling any change in your heart.'

"Before our unexpected speaker sat down, she asked if there were any who felt a change of heart during the service. A number of them raised their hands.

"I really believe that God sent this woman to give her testimony to illustrate the Bible story I told my people that Sunday."

Everything that belongs to the world--what the sinful self desires, what people see and want, and everything in this world that people are proud of--none of this comes from the Father; it all comes from the world. The world and everything in it that people desire is passing away; but he who does the will of God lives forever.

-I John 2:16, 17; The Good News Bible-

MRS. I-BELONG-TO-GOD

In Burundi, our house stood on a mountainside on the northern edge of the capital city, Bujumbura. Sundays, a hundred women and their children and some husbands came to our place for coffee and bread roll and Bible stories. Some walked many miles. They started coming at seven o'clock. When a tableful had been served, they went into the yard and sat on grass mats. By half past nine all were served, and they were ready to listen to a Bible story.

Everybody seemed glad for the cup of hot coffee. It was refreshing after the long early morning walk. But one Sunday a woman of fifty refused coffee; could she please have beer, she asked. The other women laughed at her. For nine years, she explained, she had been drinking nothing but beer, two or three bottles of it every day. She refused the bread roll, too, for beer was for her both food and drink.

On that particular day we told the story of the Prodigal Son. We were just ready to offer the closing prayer when the woman asked quite unexpectedly if she could say something.

"My stomach hurts so much," she said. "I can eat and drink nothing but beer. Would you please pray that I will be able to eat food and that I will not have so much pain?"

According to her request we remembered her in the closing prayer. She must have had a mustard seed of faith, for when the prayer was ended she responded with the words, "Imana Ishimwe," which means in the Kirundi language, "Praise the Lord."

The woman kept coming every Sunday morning, and when the Friday sewing class started, she came then too. As we got better acquainted, she told us the details of her trouble:

Contrary to our first impression, she was not an alcoholic. It was rather that beer was the only thing that she could keep on her stomach. All other food, especially non-bitter, nauseated her and would cause her to vomit soon after eating. This trouble was due to a fall she had one day when returning from hoeing in the field. From that time she started having pain on her left side. The doctors said she had to have an operation, but she was afraid because she felt she was too old for that.

She kept getting worse. We had just received a shipment of vitamins from the States and suggested she try them. She continued coming to us both Sundays and Fridays. That all her prayers seemed to go unanswered did not seem to dampen her faith.

This African woman was not without knowledge of Christianity; indeed, she was well aware of her name, Nyirakamana, which means in the Kirundi language, "I belong to God." But the political disturbances of recent years caused her to turn from religion, and when the Bible stories and the prayer of that first Sunday morning in our house broke the seven-year alienation from things religious, she herself started to pray again.

Then it happened! Just when she was beginning to think that her days on earth were few, a growth inside her passed from her in sections, and the result was transforming. Now she could eat and needed no longer to drink beer. Now she could really say "Imana Ishimwe!" Now she was telling her family and her neighbors that God did a miracle for her.

Not long afterwards, the son of Nyirakamana Imana stopped William, our interpreter, on the street to ask what that American woman did to his mother. She is so different and has become entirely well, he said. He wanted to know what kind of medicine we gave her. William replied that it was not the American woman who made his mother well. It was God.

Some days later we went to visit Mrs. I-Belong-To-God. We found her out in the field hoeing. Some of the women who had made fun of her now became believers because of her testimony.

CHANGING SHOES

Eunice Wingert

This is a story about 91 orphan children on a plane over the Pacific. They were en route from orphanages in Korea to foster parents in the United States. Miss Molly Holt, of Eugene, Oregon, was superintendent of the skyways orphanage, and was assisted by a medical doctor and eight nurses and attendants. The date was March 26, 1958.

I was one of the attendants.

The children were very young: 50 bottle babies plus 41 older tykes, none of whom were over ten years of age. Fancy the fuss and the muss of 91 children 28 hours inside a plane! There was no yard to shoo them into.

But fancy the drama of the flight! I was dead tired at flight's ending, but to have had a part in the airlifting of unwanted babies into the welcoming arms of foster parents was worth the sleepless stretch of baby-tending.

The flight was sponsored by Molly's father, Harry Holt, the Oregon farmer who became famous for his deliveries of Korean mixed-blood children to their adopting parents in the States. Since the time when he had personally selected eight infants and toddlers from Korean orphanages and by special permission from the Congress of the United States had brought them home for legal adoption into his own family, Harry Holt went into the business (non-profit, of course) of making bright futures for homeless children. By twos and fives and planeloads he airlifted them to their new worlds, a total of more than two thousand of them.

Could the flight be other than dramatic! Within that silvery shell, racing smoothly in the moonlit sky with its own bouncing shadow on the cottony clouds below, the destinies of 91 tender tiny tots were being determined. Ninety-one Orient-born "children of calamity" were farewelling irresponsible blood parents and were being Occident-reborn to Christian foster parents whom they were soon to meet at plane's landing! Ninety-one innocent children flying out of The Past and into The Future!

Of course the fifty bottle babies were quite oblivious to the meaning of what was taking place. But their unawareness only heightened the flight's drama. As I kept vigil over my eight little ones, all less than a year old, laid side by side in a basket, I could not help contrasting what is going to be with what might have been. Eight bits of babies! Will their foster parents some day tell them about this fateful flight?

But there was little time for such reflections and speculations. More immediate things like diapers and stomach aches engaged our attention. Some of the infants were on special diet. All needed close and sympathetic watching during the entire flight.

As for the older children, they were quite excited at being up so high in the air. But the drone of the motors wore them down so that by a little past midnight most of them had slipped away into dreamland. I think their dreams must have been but the extension of wakeful imaginings of what their new parents and their new homes would be like.

Our biggest problem was four-year-old Jimmy. He was a bit homesick and a good bit stubborn. The attendants took turns at consoling him. I took my turn last, and so was in for the job of dressing him up with the new American clothes in which he was to meet his foster parents. This was the last straw. To part with Korean playmates had been bad enough, and now to give up his Korean clothes was more than he could take. It required a half hour of patience and pleading before the last garment was buttoned and the last shoe tied. I was elated at my achievement.

After the twenty-eight sleepless hours came the twenty-ninth when no one *could* sleep. From all over the United States pre-screened Christian foster parents had been converging on Portland, and now that our plane was approaching the airport, we saw these waving the little strangers welcome. Dreams were about to come true. One woman, it was reported, exclaimed, "I'm going to have a baby after all!"

Looking out the window we spotted Papa Holt (everyone called him Papa!). In his arms he was holding some cartons, maybe gifts for "his children." It is said he knew the names and case histories of all the arriving young ones. He regarded -- as did also Mother Holt -- each hapless child as affectionately as though it were his very own. Although there was not enough space in the Holt farmhouse near Eugene for all "their children," crowded as it was with their own six grown children and the eight adopted mixed-bloods, the hearts of these simple folk kept enlarging with the arrival of each planeload. Harry and Bertha Holt became not only a Christian child-placing agency, but also sort of intermediate parents who gave the children their love and care until the foster parents could take over.

Our plane circled the anxious crowd and the waiting cars, landed the children gently and taxied to its stand. After some long minutes, the door opened and the attendants -- all eight of us -- left our little charges and made our exit. Then the immigration officers and Papa Holt and his crowd entered the plane and took over.

Final details in the plane took much time, in fact, an entire hour. There was an accounting of each child by the authorities and a final tidying up of the children for their entry into their new world.

To those waiting outside, the hour had a hundred minutes. When *would* the foster children be delivered into the waiting arms of their adopting parents? Standing near to the crowd, we could sense the suspense, the kind of suspense fathers-to-be have in pacing hospital hallways.

And then it happened: A Baby in arms appeared at the plane's door. A name was called. Two people moved out from the crowd to the foot of the ramp. Photographers were poised. The baby was brought down the steps. There was an ever-so-brief pause, and -- the baby was placed into the hands of the two people whose name it will bear forever.

This was it! The climax we had all looked forward to, the highlight of the flight!

But the climax was just begun. It was not ended with the handing over of the first child. The flight's climax was to be, not just a single peak, but a mountain range of peaks, a peak for each of the 90 children still inside the plane.

Papa Holt, his arms still unlowered, stood smiling as he watched the first enlarged family melt back into the crowd.

Then into those arms was put another baby. Again a name was called. And again two people came forward to receive the child.

And then a third . . .

And a fourth . . .

One after another Papa Holt handed over the children. It was like giving out prizes. Already several dozen pairs of parents, surrounded by envious friends, were examining their "prizes" in out-of-the-way places around the airport. All other eyes were focused on the destiny-determining drama being played out at the plane's door.

And the twenty-fourth!

And the fortieth!

There was Pansy, youngest of all the children. She was just three weeks old. I had helped watch over the tiny thing and now was happy to note how very kind the adopting parents seemed as they walked away with the little bundle. "She looks Korean, and I would have been disappointed had it been otherwise," the foster mother said.

Three-year-old Harry fared extra well. He got not only new parents, but also a new brother, a playmate who would help him to learn the new ways in his new home.

A number of attendants noticed that the faces of some of the older children were dirty as they came out of the plane. Did we not wash them clean when we dressed them before landing? On close examination the truth became known; it was chocolate bars Papa Holt had had in those boxes under his arms when he entered the plane.

And Jasmin! Papa Holt took a lot of time when it came to Jasmin's turn. The beautiful ten-year-old was his pet. Oldest of the group, she had been a little mother to the younger children already back there in the Korean orphanage, and was Molly's "little assistant" on the just-ended flight. Papa Holt lifted her off her feet into his strong farmer's arms, gave her a hug, and, reluctant-like, handed her over to her lucky foster parents.

The height of the climax peaks in the day's proceedings varied with the different individuals and the different circumstances. For Papa Holt, as we have just noted, the highest peak was Jasmin. For me it was Jimmy.

My tussle with the maddening but nevertheless lovable tyke had stimulated the special interest, and I watched for his appearance. "Look," someone cried before I noticed, "that boy has on two different kinds of shoes!" Sure enough, it was Jimmy, and he did have on a Korean shoe and an American one. During his long waiting period inside the plane, the little fellow had apparently succeeded in removing one of his new shoes and replacing it with his old one. Although only a half-success (he got the string knotted up on the other western shoe), he had an air of victory that seemed to say, "See, I won after all."

I conceded defeat. But my thoughts went deeper. Aren't Jimmy's shoes a symbol of the mixed blood and dual nationality of these children? Born of Korean mothers and adopted by Americans, they belong to two countries. How confusing to these young lives this half-and-halfness!

I think, furthermore, that Jimmy with the two different kinds of shoes on his feet was saying something like this: "Please take it easy. Let me make the changeover gradually. Let me have the familiar feel of one of my old shoes while I get used to the complicated western ones.

Later on, then, I'll go all-out for the western shoes."

The foster parents accepted Jimmy "as is." Their understanding attitude seemed to say, "We *will* take it easy, sonnyboy!"

Came the eighty-fifth child . . .

By now the crowd around the plane was diminishing. Knots of people with a child in the midst were everywhere. Parents were selling themselves to their children.

Fifteen minutes and five children more -- and the plane was empty.

But there were still two pairs of parents who had not received a child, and the count was ninety. Where were the other two children?

Actually there were to have been 92 children on the plane. Just minutes before takeoff in Seoul, the ninety-second child, Betty, was taken from the group by her mother who had decided at that late moment she wanted her baby after all. Said the disappointed mother magnanimously, "If Betty's real mother wanted to keep her, it was better so." Betty is still wearing Korean shoes.

The other missing child was Baby Alice. Somewhere high over the Pacific the little girl had decided that one year of "unwanted" earthly life was enough. She had accepted an invitation from the angels to slip out of the plane to play with them among the stars. The plane's doctor had tried vainly to induce her to go along back to earth, but she was already gone far out into the Milky Way. Only her tiny body returned to earth to rest there in the native soil of her unknown father. The intended foster parents had been apprised of the situation minutes after arrival. Baby Alice was wearing neither Korean sandals nor American shoes; she had chosen golden slippers.

To each of the disappointed parents Papa Holt promised another baby another time.

And so the flight was ended. Cars were now fanning out to nearly half of the States in the Union. For 90 children the die was cast; they had exchanged a life of ostracism in Korea for a life of worth and respectability in America.

Years hence, a greying father will one day open an attic trunk, pull out a rubber shoe, and relate the details of a story only dimly remembered by his son. And that night son James will fervently thank God for the divine love and human concern that planned and brought about that fateful Pacific flight.

CLOUDBURST IN CALCUTTA

Come with me to India. It is Monday, June 13, 1960. I've just arrived in Calcutta from Bangkok, Thailand on my round-the-world photographic mission. I had not informed the India MCC Director the exact time of my arrival. I have the address, but not his telephone number. Threatening black clouds give me a dark reception. I wait for half an hour while a ten-year-old urchin scurries around the airport to find a taxi for me. He finally finds a dilapidated one and is pleased with the half-rupee in his hand.

Now get into the old taxi with me. We haven't driven fifteen minutes when we are stopped with a cloudburst. We aren't sure if the driver, who doesn't speak English, knows where he is going; at least he has a paper on which an airport official has written directions for him.

The cloudburst now abates into a heavy rain, and we are driving again, slowly, through flooded streets. The water gets deeper, comes up through the floorboards of the car. We continue driving at a snail's pace, block after block, street after street in central Calcutta. The streets are filled with water and the water is filled with people, rickshaws, trucks and stalled cars. There is bedlam. Outside the car windows is a seething humanity. I put up the windows all the way to make the pale-face American less accessible. I breathe a prayer which God answers with a miraculous calm in my heart. Our motor conks out. Our laughing driver dries out the carburetor with a rag. Gangs of men pushing cars push us also. We sit with our feet on the top of the front seat. I wonder if the baggage in the trunk is getting wet. I envy the rickshaw riders who pass us. A big truck goes by and sends waves of water into our car. Now the motor starts again, goes a block, stops again. The dense Calcutta population is having a sort of carnival time in the water-filled streets. We still do not know if the driver knows where he is going, and we have serious doubts if he'll get there. The motor starts again and conks out again.

For two full hours we've been stopping and starting and praying. Then the water gradually subsides, and by the ascending house numbers we know we are outbound from the city's center. A half hour more of erratic driving, and then we see in the evening dusk, thank God, the miracle of the triple-letter sign, "MCC." We draw a sigh of relief, but not for long. As we come nearer, we find the building closed. Only the dog is home, and there is a sign, "Beware the dog!"

A crowd gathers round. One man indicates by signs he knows where the people live. He gets into the taxi, and we drive for ten minutes more. The sacred cows don't know about our worries; they don't even look up as we pass them. Finally we stop, and our guide points to a door. I ring the bell at the door and it is one of the high points of my entire trip when we see the welcome faces of Vernon and Helen Reimer.

The taxi fare? I couldn't believe it -- two dollars!

Look out for one another's interests, not just for your own.

-Philippians 2:4, The Good News Bible-

THIS IS GOD

by Yoshitaka Yamamoto
(Our Japanese helper in Tokyo)

I must tell you what I have found at MCC and what my purpose is for the future.

It was really my turning point in life when I found MCC. If anyone asks me, "What is the most important thing in the pathway of our lives?" I will answer him without hesitation, "It is to find God."

In exchange for the kindness which MCC has shown to me, I would like to tell you what I have experienced as an MCC helper at Ueno Park, a slum section in Tokyo, in recent months.

Although Japan is a small country, we Japanese traditionally like to travel. We like to get out of the city and converse with nature. Tokyo people like to get out once a month to escape from the hurry and bustle of city life.

There are some, however, who seldom get out of the city. They are the ragpickers and other homeless people whom we see at Ueno Park. They travel, yes, but only as they tramp the dusty city streets to hunt for rags and old paper.

Many look upon these poor and homeless people as being wicked, or as hermits who isolate themselves from society, a group of folk who can hardly be called normal people. But by picking out an experience I had recently, I wish to show how lovely even these people can be, and how God gives His blessing to the poorest of them.

One Friday evening I approached some ragpickers who were making a blazing fire. I met them with a smile, ready for the milk distribution as usual. It seemed to me that the many officers, workers, students and tourists who were rambling about were all filled with joy, peace and hope. In sharp contrast, how lonely and unhappy these homeless people seemed! It made me feel sad. It made me bitter. Before God, should not everyone be the same? I said to myself. But I suppressed my anger which was rising from the bottom of my heart because of this contradiction of things, and I passed out some printed sheets of the hymn, "What a Friend We Have in Jesus."

Then we sang together. We sang out of tune. Some of the voices were like those of bullfrogs. But we sang.

> What a Friend we have in Jesus, all our sins and griefs to bear;
> What a privilege to carry everything to God in prayer;

O what peace we often forfeit; O what needless pain we bear,
All because we do not carry everything to God in prayer.

Truly, they evidenced in their hearty singing that they wanted to find this True Friend. Then we thanked God for the milk and served it as usual.

Just as I started to go home, I noticed a well-dressed lady, about 25 years of age, standing behind us. Without hesitation, she came up and started to talk with us. She told us the following story with tears in her eyes:

"Just three years ago I was in this park as a prostitute. I was a poor prostitute living from hand to mouth. When I could not get any guest, I could not pay even my room rent. I had only one warm, helping hand. It was Oji-san, a tea-stall keeper. Whenever I did not know what to do, I would go to Oji-san and borrow some money, or would eat his rice without paying for it. No matter how often I came, he always welcomed me to his stall. I began to think it was just natural to receive food from someone else. In fact, I was not much better than an animal.

"But it was through Oji-san that I came to my senses, and through whom I was born again to a new life.

"One rainy day as I was passing by Oji-san's, he called to me, 'Sei-chan, Sei-chan, come in!' I went in. He served me a cup of hot green tea as usual, and then he began to speak seriously:

" 'Winter is near at hand,' he said. 'I have to close my stall during the winter and go back to Kamakura where my son lives.'

"Still more seriously he said, 'I am a Christian. When I was young I tried to become rich by any means, but my efforts all resulted in failure. I have learned many lessons. After I became a Christian I wanted to work for the Lord and lay up my treasures in Heaven as much as possible. Of course, I have made many mistakes. But I have found one great truth: it is that we should always lend a helping hand to those who are poor.'

"With tender eyes he looked at me and said, 'Sei-chan, it seems to me that you are surrounded by the angels which God has sent to you. In fact, just as you can see me, so you will also be able to see the angels if you but open your eyes which God gives you, for everywhere the angels fly around us always."

"As he spoke these words, something like a vision occurred to me. I saw my parents in my native district. I saw them working hard from morning till evening. Although I did not see the angels, I did then and there decide to go back home. Oji-san gave me my train fare. Oji-san also gave me something else, something much better than train fare. It was a Bible.

"What was it that was waiting for me when I got back home? Neither my parents nor our neighbors proved to be the 'angels' I had expected. They were not friendly toward a girl who had been a prostitute.

"In spite of it all, I continued to believe Oji-san's words. I put my best thoughts, my best work, my best energy into everything I did in order to find the angels whom Oji-san told me about.

"This morning I came to Ueno Park to see Oji-san. But I learned that he had died almost a year ago. I was so much disappointed. But now that he is in Heaven he can still see that I have been new-born."

After this speech, she took out some cakes from her furoshiki and distributed them to the ragpickers freely, cakes which she had perhaps intended to give to Oji-san as a gift. And then she gave some money to a few prostitutes who are in the same predicament as she was three years ago.

I wanted to know where she lives and what she is doing now. But she was lost in the crowd without telling me anything more, not even her family name.

The ragpickers and prostitutes who were listening to her could say nothing. Her words had impressed them deeply. And at that moment I could not help but cry out, "THIS IS GOD!"

I kept thinking about her all the way home, and I was so happy.

Truly, Christ is the Way, the Truth and the Life I have experienced through His Divine Word. Each of us pursues a different way, but we young people should know and keep in mind that wealth is nothing, position is nothing and God is everything. With God everything is possible!

THEY TAUGHT THEIR ENEMIES TO SEW

In the very heart of Africa live tall and slender tribespeople called Watutsi. They raise cattle that look like Texas longhorns. They are not farmers, but make the people of another tribe provide them with food. For hundreds of years the tall Watutsi have made the shorter people, the farmers, serve them like slaves. The slave tribespeople are called Bahutus.

About four years ago the shorter people became angry at having to work so hard for their tall masters and rose in revolt against them. With long spears, axes and machetes, they killed thousands of them.

Some of the Watutsi had become Christians through the influence of Protestant Christian missions in their country and as a result treated the Bahutu more kindly than did those who were not Christians. But when the Bahutu farmer slaves rose up in rebellion against the Watutsi, they showed little mercy, and thus the Watutsi Christians suffered with the rest. Some of them were killed. Others had to flee into other countries as refugees.

In one of these countries to which many thousands of these tall refugees fled, there were some Mennonite Central Committee relief workers who were distributing food and clothing and medicines in the name of Christ to whoever needed help most. When the refugees started to come, the relief workers felt that these homeless people were still more needy than others and so reached out helping hands to them.

One of the ways in which the relief workers helped the Watutsi refugees was by teaching young women to sew. Christian people sent sewing machines and large amounts of materials in the name of Christ with which the girls could make clothing for themselves and for others. After about six months a class of ten Watutsi young women had learned to sew sufficiently well to become teachers themselves.

Now there is a very unusual angle to this story.

It would be quite natural for the Watutsi refugee sewing teachers to want to help their own tribespeople. Having been homeless themselves, they would naturally want to help others who are homeless. It would be quite another matter, would it not, if they had to teach people who belonged to their enemy tribe, the Bahutu?

But that is exactly what the Watutsi young women agreed to do. All the members of the new sewing class were cripples and belonged to the Bahutu tribe.

How could they do it? How could they be helping their enemies? Only one hundred miles away, Bahutus were still killing Watutsi.

The answer is that this is the way Christianity works. The refugee young women had learned more than just how to sew during their six-months course. They had caught some of the atmosphere in the relief center. They had been impressed by the demonstration of a Christian love that caused people far away to send teachers and materials to help them to learn to sew. In the devotional periods at the center, they had learned about Jesus. They had learned to pray. Some of them believed in Jesus as their Savior. This is why they were now ready to pass on kindnesses which they had received to others, even to those who were their enemies.

Did I not weep for him that was in trouble? Was not my soul grieved for the poor?

-Job 30:25, The King James Version-

A DANISH CHRISTMAS IN AFRICA

We have experienced Christmas in America, in Germany, in Austria, in Japan and in Hong Kong, but never have we enjoyed one so unique as that of 1962 at a lone Danish Baptist mission station high up on the tablelands of Central Africa. It was really two celebrations: Christmas Eve in the home of the Danish missionary family and Christmas Morn in the mission's African church.

The Christmas tree in the Danish home had wax candles, not electric imitations. Like in America, the presents lay under the tree. Christmas dinner was eaten on Christmas Eve. Danish custom prescribed red cabbage, rice, potatoes, and three kinds of meat. In the dish of dry rice were hidden two almond nuts, the finders of which were entitled to two colorful packages of bonbons on the table. After dinner, letters and presents were opened, and then all joined hands in ring-around-the-tree singing of Danish carols.

I once went to sleep to the tinkling of cowbells on a Swiss mountainside. It is amazing how far the tinkling carries on a still, starlit night. Here, too, on this Christmas Eve night, I again heard the tone of a bell that was sounding as far and clear over African mountains as did the cowbells in Switzerland. It was half past two, and the measured soundings of the gong were calling Africans from their grass huts to a Christmas candlelight service in the mission church scheduled for four o'clock.

I cannot convey to you the magic of that night. As we walked to the church, the stars were shining crisp and bright in the rarefied air of a 7,000-foot elevation. The Dipper was there, and just above it the Morning Star. The brilliant star was standing just over the church, and we so easily imagined ourselves on the way to Bethlehem. Literally it was "Silent Night!"

We arrived at the church a few minutes before four o'clock. We found it already filled. How and when the people got there I do not know, for we had heard no commotion. Dozens of little candles were lighting the church. Some of them were on the tree, some were scattered throughout the church on sprigs of holly.

We were shown places at the front of the church near the Christmas tree; indeed, so near that one of the branches, on which was a candle, was to stroke my face all during the program. By the light of the candles, we now surveyed the audience that we were facing. Both adults and children sat there almost statue-like. We noticed that some were very poorly dressed, some better, a few elegantly.

It was not the people who at this stage engaged our major attention; it was the quiet, the stillness, both inside the church and out, that bore in on our souls. For five long minutes it lasted. Then a lever clicked, and Christmas carols from a battery-powered record player filled the room.

So it was nearly half past four when the program proper began. There were Scripture readings, prayers, messages and musical numbers that lasted until daybreak. The program had been well-planned, and it moved along smoothly, all of it in the Kirundi language. Most unusual number was that of a mothers' choir; they all had children either in their arms or on their backs while they sang.

Before the main Christmas message, I brought greetings to the group. "Christians in many lands are rejoicing with you today," I said, "and you must know that you are not alone in your faith in Christ; you belong to a large group of believers around the world, and are included in the 'whosoever' of John 3:16 who have the promise of everlasting life."

With closing prayer came the break of day. By the time the sun appeared over the horizon, most of these friendly African Christians were returning to their grass hut homes.

A VISIT TO LILLIAN DICKSON'S HOSPITAL

Orie Miller was on the move again. As executive secretary of MCC, he was boarding plane for another round-the-world administrative visit. His first stop would be Taiwan. Two months earlier he had requested that I, then one year into our Japanese assignment, should meet him in Taiwan for the cornerstone laying for a hospital at Hwalien on August 21, 1954. For a week, Orie surveyed the on-going MCC program on the island, and then accompanied me in my return to Japan.

Besides taking lessons from the MCC Taiwan operation, I had the privilege during that week to visit Lillian Dickson's famed 750-bed leprosarium, 15 miles out of Taipei. Lillian herself served as interpreter between the leprosy patients and me.

I was deeply impressed in our visit to the "hopeless ward." Lillian was showing me a hundred broken bodies that the killer had already gnawed upon to the stage of no return. There they lay, or sat squatting on their straw-matted wooden bunks! A few of the less deformed were shuffling through the hallways. All of them were waiting for the *coup de grace* which was to fall tomorrow, or next week, or at best, next year. Properly, indeed, was the building that housed these living corpses called the "hopeless ward!"

For a broody few this hopelessness pervaded soul as well as body. There was no hope for this life nor for the life that was to begin at coming painful death. Theirs was utter and total hopelessness! No wonder they refused to respond to the presence of guests! Numb and gloomy, they held no more interest in the clean world outside; they were past redemption!

For others among them, the hopelessness applied only to their rotting bodies; it did not reach into their faith-protected souls. We could spot them easily. As we moved from room to room, they called to us, "penang!" (the Christian greeting meaning "peace"). The greeting was sometimes plainly articulated, sometimes mumbled through distorted mouths. We knew their eyes were smiling, even though they looked at us with scary stares. Plainly, they were happy to see us, especially her whom they had come to love and who they knew loved them.

In one room three men picked up their homemade banjos and played with their finger stubs, "Take it to the Lord in prayer." And in the corner of the same room, a suffering prostrate form asked us to pray for him. "I have such constant pain," he said, pointing to his bandaged foot, and then he added with the trace of a smile, "The pain is all in my foot, praise God, there's none in my heart." One could almost hear the leprosy gnawing at his already toeless foot. But one could also sense the joy and peace that was dwelling in his soul. Lillian Dickson and I were here witnessing the drama of spiritual triumph in the midst of corporeal devastation.

Had there remained any trace of doubt that Christian faith enables one to meet the worst of life's crises victoriously, Iu-sensei was one whose story would have dissolved even that.

A former Chinese schoolteacher, Iu-sensei was squatting on his mat near to the one with the aching foot. The facial skin was smooth and shiny and tautly drawn. His teeth showed conspicuously. One leg was missing. What a sight for an intelligent, degreed educator!

Now we were standing beside his bunk. He was speaking animatedly in a mumbled Chinese which Lillian Dickson managed to understand and pass along to me in English:

"You should know," he said by way of explanation, "what an atmosphere of despair was in this place some years ago. We leper patients lay on the bare boards of these wooden bunks. Wounds were unbandaged and we got cold. Several boards in my bunk got broken and they would not fix it. I lay helplessly on these jagged boards while rats would come to chew at my back and legs. Seldom a day went by without a suicide. Sometimes there were as many as three. I, too, tried to take my life -- five times -- but without success. Is it strange that one should try to take one's life when one is in such great pain and when there's not a single friend who cares? Who but we can comprehend such bitter hopelessness!"

He continued, "One day a visitor came into our ward and showed herself friendly. When she left, she said she would come again. I was sure she wouldn't. And so were all the others. Visitors do not come here more than once. There is danger they'll get leprosy. When they do come, they do so out of morbid curiosity."

Iu-sensei brightened up. "But she fooled us. She did come back, not merely once, but many times. And she didn't come alone; she brought with her some straw mats for us to lay on and blankets to keep us warm. Here was someone from the outside who cared.

"The effect on us was electric. The number of suicides fell off. Those of us who had had Christian faith found a new assurance. The unbelievers among us were deeply impressed. Her coming turned me to a really vital Christian faith.

"The time had come for a third amputation on my leg. This time it must be high above the knee. At least, so the doctor said. But I had other thoughts. Why not amputate the affected flesh below the knee, and ask God to stop the disease? I had lost all confidence in the doctor's ability to stop the leprosy, and our visitor's advice and example inspired me to believe God would do it. I asked for a Christian doctor to take the place of the one who persisted in urging the amputation above the knee. My request was granted, and together we prayed that the disease might be stayed. He amputated according to my request."

And then, had it not been disfigured, Iu-sensei's face would really have beamed as he joyfully announced, "That was six months ago. Three months after the operation, my leg was completely healed, and there has been no return of any lesion. God performed a miracle. He answered my prayer. The normal course of leprosy had reversed itself, and instead of getting progressively worse, it has been permanently arrested. Every day I am rejoicing and thanking God."

Just before we left, Iu-sensei remarked something to his fellow Christians, and then said to Lillian Dickson, "Tell him (meaning me) we will be praying for him on his round-the-world trip."

And could I answer other than that I too will be remembering all of them in my prayers!

Lillian Dickson requested I preach to the 200 Christians who were able to come to the leprosarium's Evangelical Church the following Sunday. Since there were two interpreters, one for the Mainland Chinese and one for the Taiwanese, I had much time to think between the rounds of thought-transfer. So impressed was I that not long afterwards I expressed my thoughts into the following poem:

TWO WAY SERMON

I saw two hundred lepers near Taipei today.
They sat before me in a church, down there away
From elevated pulpit chair where I surveyed
The crippled congregation ere we prayed.

Then I, the clean, with two interpreters between,
Did speak the words of life to them who were unclean.
Mainland Chinese and Taiwanese in turn did hear
The English words transferred to sounds that fit their ear.

It took three times as long as usual to speak.
Between the rounds of lingual thought-transfer there streaked
Into my soul such moving meditations rare
As made me silent breathe a simultaneous prayer:

"What is it, Lord, that I have done or have not done
That I deserve to stand up here with every one
Of body members whole, while they to whom I speak
Down there do have such ghastly, painful-scarred physique?"

"You don't! You don't deserve," methought I heard God say,
"Your health. As though you think My blessings are for pay!
Your lungs and legs and ears and eyes are gifts from Me;
I should be thanked when you can breathe and run and hear and see!

"And as for these to whom you do now speak, they're Mine;
You cannot see the details of My wise design.
Be grateful, son, for uncontaminated health,
But, too, trust Me to bless this leper commonwealth."

Of th' all-sufficiency of Christ I spoke today,
And while I preached, the congregation seemed to say
A meaningful amen; in fact, preached back to me
Impressive proof of what a Christian life can be.

And then it seemed to me that with an X-ray view
I saw through th' unclean bodies sitting in the pew
To cleansed hearts that shone as pure as flesh showed vile,
And *knew* the reason why they worshipped with a smile.

THREE WAYS TO GIVE

Brushing away theological niceties, I pose the simple proposition that Christianity is *giving*, and conversely, giving is Christianity.

To give is Christian. God gave and He still gives. Jesus gave and gives. Giving is a law of life; it is a law of God. The apple gives up its form and its beauty when it is eaten. The mother gives herself to her child.

Conversely, the selfish Christian *gets.* But what a contradictory term: a selfish Christian! Each of these two words cancels out the other.

But face it we must, must we not? Everyone of us has somewhere between a speck and a peck of selfishness in him. We do like to *get*.

For some, getting is the passion of their lives. Friends of John D. Rockefeller intimately said his face never lit up except when he learned of an opportunity to turn a dollar. The biographer of Paul Getty, the richest living American, uses such expressions regarding Getty as: "his bold appetite for buying and selling; his passion for grasping."

It was only Jesus who poured out His soul unto death. Not a single miracle did He ever perform for His own benefit. If, on the one hand, it has been the passion of some men's lives to get, on the other hand, it was the passion of our Lord's life to give. He and He only is the ideal Giver.

I would like to suggest three kinds of giving:

The first is *thing-giving*. It is the lowest rung in the giving-ladder. It is really easy for us to give what we can spare of our own material possessions. We like to share as long as there is plenty left. Sometimes, though, it takes a social pressure even in our spare giving. We put a dollar into the collection plate, even though secretly we would like to keep it; it wouldn't look good if we didn't. We invite the Smiths to dinner because the Smiths had us a month ago.

Giving becomes still more difficult when bank accounts are low and pocketbooks near empty. Our homes are of course equipped with the modern conveniences, but these are necessities, and it would really be hard to choose which one to give up. What I'm trying to say is that it is surprising how tightly glued we do become to material possessions and the easy life.

At first we possess our possessions, but with the increase of accessions to our possessions, prepossessions of ownership become obsessions, and we're possessed by our possessions.

It is not to compare ourselves with each other; we must compare ourselves with the ideal Giver, with Him who gave Himself poor that we might become rich. Even in our generousness, we become ashamed when we consider Him.

> I know not why God gave me bounteous store,
> While others eat their rice on earthen floor;
> I know not why I should have more than they
> Unless He meant that I should give a part away.

The second rung in the giving-ladder is *self-giving*.

Longfellow's idea of giving one's self with the gift isn't the easiest to carry out. I found this to be true in my own experience as a relief worker. To send out notices to "come and get it," to open doors at nine, to shove the stuff across the counter with an I'm-sorry-but-I-don't-have-time-to-talk-with-you air, to wash one's hands at five, to eat dinner, and then to curl up in an easy chair with one's favorite magazine -- this is not too difficult an assignment.

But to listen to one tragic story after another, to "rejoice with them that rejoice and weep with them that weep," to try genuinely to do something about bearing another's burdens -- this requires considerable second-mile-ism.

To make one's self sympathetically available to all comers disarranges also one's neatly-arranged daily schedules. It takes a super-sweet temper to bear up under such repeated frustrations. We didn't know the meaning of that word, *frustrations,* until we went to Africa. But really, should Christians not care about people? If one does genuinely care about people -- hungry people, homeless people, ugly people, sinful people, vexing people, lovable people, Christian people, problem people, harmful people -- all this adds pain to the Christian life. For one cannot care without suffering. Immediately you enter into the agonies of those who need you, and you feel with these people to the extent that some of their sorrows, at least, become your own.

Here, again, I must admit my shortcomings. I am pretty much interested in *my* welfare, *my* program, *my* duties, *my* comfort. I have a great deal of "I" trouble. It gets in the way when I'm helping others.

The top rung in the giving-ladder goes beyond both thing-giving and *self-giving*. Beyond the food and friendliness and medicines, beyond the reach of all human helping hands and hearts, there remain unfilled needs. For these superhuman needs there must be a superhuman answer. That answer is He who said, "All power is given unto Me," and who proclaimed the blessed invitation, "Come unto ME all ye that are heavy laden and I will give you rest!"

It is the Christian's highest privilege of all to share this good news and to recommend this answer to all who have problems beyond the reach of human help. Isn't it criminal for all who profess to be Christians not to tell the good news that God forgives sins and offers eternal life for the taking, and that God gives the ballast necessary to hold one's ship steady? As one of our helpers in Austria said, "I think it is our duty to pull the curtains from their windows so that light comes in, and when sunshine does touch their shy eyes, let's pray, 'O Father, let them see, let them feel what unconsciously they seek -- You and Your Peace!' "

Human hands rolled away the stone and unwound the graveclothes, but it took the divine command of the Master to restore life to Lazarus, and a relief program can become a re-life program only when human giving is supplemented by divine Omnipotence.

Thing-giving, self-giving, gospel-giving! Now let us erase the divisions, and see only the *giving Christian*. There stands Christ Jesus, our Lord! See Him in the beauty of His humility, hear His compassionate words from the cross, behold the ideal Giver, the unlimited Lover! He is our Challenge, our Ideal toward which we strive!

THE TALE OF THREE DAUGHTERS

While working with the Mennonite Central Committee in Japan and Hong Kong from 1953 to 1960, we acquired three "daughters," two Japanese, one Chinese. The stories of the three girls follow:

RACHEL: In Tokyo we met Koko whose Christian name was Rachel. Rachel was mainstay and interpreter at our Open House events when 50 Japanese youth met for three days of playing, praying and studying.

At Ueno Park, a Tokyo slum then, Rachel helped with a feeding project. Unashamedly she was witness to her faith to ragpickers, drugpushers and passersby. Although she attended Bible classes, her family was Buddhist.

When a typhoon struck Kyushu, Japan's southernmost island, MCC allotted $1,000 for flood relief. Rachel urged her father, a manufacturer of *futons* (Japanese style comforters) to also do something for the disaster victims. He sent two truckloads of futons to the disaster area and Rachel herself helped to distribute them.

Rachel still keeps a correspondence with her American "Pop and Mom." She is now married and has two daughters, Kae, 17, and Chikako, 12. Although her husband, a gas station operator, is not a Christian, he encourages her in her faith.

KEIKO: Keiko lived in Yamaguchi Ken, the area where the American bomb fell on Hiroshima. Life at home was unhappy for her. At 16 she left for Tokyo where she became a floater in a city of eight million. Missionary Peter Willms, who knew her family, wrote us a note: "We gave Keiko your MCC address," Peter said, "and urge that you give her help if and when she comes to you."

After many hardships, Keiko came. We made her a member of our MCC Tamagawa Center family. The contrast between her family and the Christian atmosphere was revolutionary for her. In no time at all she responded to the gospel story and learned to speak English well. She was "Mom's" constant helper in the kitchen and the Ueno distributions, and she assisted "Pop" in serving cups of milk to the many unemployed outside the city labor office. She and some Christian girl friends started a neighborhood Sunday School in the MCC garage.

Keiko lived with us for almost two years, and when her family demanded that she return home to marry a man of their choosing, she obeyed. Japanese custom decrees that parents be obeyed.

Keiko kept in touch with us by mail. She said she got work in an American PX store, and there met a Christian American soldier, whom she came to love. Her family, however, insisted on a Buddhist husband. After long spiritual struggle, she decided against her family's wish, married the Christian soldier and was ostracized by her family.

The couple came to the United States where both of them were graduated from Christian college. Her husband continued his training for a master's degree in Los Angeles Biola Seminary. Today they both teach in Placentia, California, have three children and are active in church work. Several times they have entertained us in their lovely home. They still hope to return some day to Japan as missionaries.

Recently Keiko's husband gave her a trip to Japan to visit her family. When she phoned her family on arrival, her mother said she did not want to see her. But Keiko went in spite of the refusal. After several days her mother remarked, "Keiko, what has happened to you? You seem so happy." Keiko returned to the United States rejoicing she had communicated the gospel story to her mother.

JASMIN: Jasmin's family lived in famous Nathan Road, Kowloon, Hong Kong. When MCC transferred us to the British colony after four years in Japan it was this Chinese family who shared their living quarters with us in that overcrowded city. Jasmin's father was an offical in the Hong Kong government. Her mother spoke only Cantonese and Mandarin.

Jasmin, 16, was the counterpart in Hong Kong of Rachel and Keiko in Japan. Because she spoke excellent English she served as interpreter and helped with the distributions at Kwong Wah Charity Hospital in Kowloon where an average of 63 babies were born every day. To Jasmin we were her "American Grandpa and Grandma."

About a year after our transfer to Hong Kong from Japan, Rachel visited us there and became a close friend of Jasmin.

Just before we left Hong Kong we sent Jasmin to Upland College Academy, Upland, California, where she had the honor of being voted by the student body as the one who contributed most to the spiritual life of the school. Later, Jasmin transferred to Azusa College, Azusa, California, where she earned a bachelor's degree.

By the time of her graduation, Jasmin's student visa was running out. We drove to Los Angeles to assist her in securing a permanent visa for the United States. We noticed an unusually broad smile, and she finally told us that the night before she had become engaged to a young Christian Taiwanese who had a valid resident's visa. This solved Jasmin's visa problems.

Today this couple and their little son Jeffry live in Sepulveda, a suburb of Los Angeles. They give much time to Christian work.

REUNION: In 1976, we received a letter from Rachel: "Dear my American Pop and Mom! My husband is making it possible for me and my two daughters to visit you in August. I can't believe my dream is coming true!"

On August 11, 1976, Keiko and Jasmin and their husbands greeted Rachel at the Los Angeles airport, and two days later, after a 20-year separation, "Mom and Pop" came from Reedley for a reunion in the Upland Brethren in Christ Church.

Our own daughter Lois and her husband Robert, who had followed us in a Japan assignment, chaired the evening of reminiscing by conversation and photographs. The reminiscing naturally turned into thanksgiving and praise to God for the bonds of Christian fellowship forged through MCC's concern in these Asian lands.

CHARLOTTE

Charlotte was a 24-year-old Jewess whose home had been in Czechoslovakia. During the Hitler regime, all the members of her family were cremated in a concentration camp. Charlotte herself had to carry wood for the ovens. She experienced in reality what is usually the stuff of the most frightful nightmares. She escaped the common fate of the Auschwitz holocaust only by the timely arrival of the American Army.

Thus miraculously released, Charlotte became a stateless refugee in Switzerland. God brought her and Mrs. Wingert together on a train near Basel. Through a series of providence, Charlotte, at the moment of this writing, is on her way to a new home with the Marshall Wingers in Canada.

The Basel MCC Center invited Charlotte to dinner just before sailing. Wrote Charlotte: "Now begins in me a new life, a life with purpose, and I am expecting all my dreams to be consummated in fulfillment. What unusual things take place in life! One can really say that there are miracles in the world, and unhappiness can come so unexpectedly. The people to whom I am going must be very good, since they take so much interest in an entire stranger. I can only thank the dear God for everything, for my words are much too dull, even if I say thank-you a thousand times."

UPDATE: It was on Charlotte's trip to Canada that she disappeared into thin air. We had secured a valid passport and visa for her, and arranged for her safe embarkation. At the same time we had informed the Winger family the date of her arrival at Montreal, but somewhere, somehow, Charlotte disappeared en route. Although Rev. Winger appeared at the appointed time and place to meet her, the doubly unfortunate girl failed to show up. Just what happened to her will no doubt never be known. It is known that she disembarked at Montreal, but investigation yielded no trace of her. She may have been kidnapped, or she may have changed her mind en route (which is quite unlikely), or she may have been persuaded by Jewish travelers to go with them. It was indeed a severe blow to us that this lovely girl who had suffered so much should have to experience this second tragedy.

CREEDS, NEEDS AND DEEDS

It takes a longtime stay in the Orient for one to become fully aware of what the present-day plenty has done to us of the West. Unconsciously, luxury softens the body and hardens the heart. We are blissfully unaware of the wide and deep chasm between our standard of living and that of the masses. Even when the tourist does see, he doesn't. It is impossible, or nearly so, for him who has never known want to imaginatively project himself sympathetically and vicariously into the day-to-day, year-to-year existence of the have-nots; he just looks across the chasm with a "too bad!" objectivity. Living on "easy street" insidiously desensitizes the heart. Western Christians, professed followers of the lowly Nazarene, are not aware of the creeping paralysis of materialism. It is possible for even relief workers to wade knee-deep through human needs and be so interested in souvenirs and Kodachromes that the pain does not reach the heart.

In saying this, I'm not only preaching; I'm also confessing. How difficult it is to project one's self into the lives of others, to rejoice, to hope, to suffer with them, to help their burdens. After all, don't I have concerns of my own; haven't I the right to live my own life! Even after six years of experience in relief work, it seems I'm still in the primer stage of selfless living. I see vistas of poured-out-ness to which I have not attained. The Master still challenges me to *follow* Him, to demonstrate my creed and to match the needs I see with deeds.

This awareness of slowness in learning God's school of selfless living is made more acute by examples He has been sending across my path. There was Uncle Robert of Austria! There was Prillie, of Germany! And now, in Japan, I am shamed and challenged by still other unselfish lives, this time those of our very own MCC household. It is as though the Lord were saying to me: "See, I am demonstrating right under your nose what I mean by having a *living* faith. Go, translate, like they, your creeds to deeds; go share, like they, yourself and your store with those in need; give that which is in your hand; *follow* Me!"

The story of one of our MCC helpers will illustrate what I mean:

Sometime ago Shiba-san, 27 and single, came to the MCC center. He had been excommunicated from a monastery after two years as a novitiate.

He told us he could no longer conscientiously subscribe to some of the doctrines of his church. He asked many questions and wanted to know if there were others who believed as he regarding certain doctrines.

The young man was friendless and homeless. His father, mother, a brother and a sister had been killed in a Tokyo bombing. He now had no place to go. He was penniless, hungry and emaciated from the rigors of monastic life.

He asked for nothing. In agony of spirit he was debating the one question: Should he break with his church? He had just two weeks in which to decide. Either he must untruthfully resubscribe to its doctrines and be received into the fold, or stay away permanently.

We sensed the sincerity of this young man and invited him to stay for the night. He did -- that night and every night since.

Shiba-san has been reorienting himself to this new life. He is quiet, cultured, happy and has been helpful in the kitchen, Sunday School and the distributions at Ueno and Shibuya. He gave short gospel messages several times.

His attitude bespeaks his gratefulness for the food and clothing he receives but he never asks for favors.

Until recently he received only such cash as was necessary for this rehabilitation, such as for haircuts and dental work. Then one day we gave him a 1,000-yen note ($2.78) in appreciation for the help he has been to MCC and suggested he get with it whatever he wished, maybe to buy himself a shirt.

It was his turn that morning to supervise early milk distribution. We gave him 200 yen for taxi fare to take the kettles and cups from Shibuya distribution center to the Mishiku center and suggested he then take the day off to do whatever he wished.

Shiba-san went on a spending spree that day, but quite a different spree than one would guess. He went downtown after the milk distribution and purchased as much bread as the money would buy. He took the bread to homeless and hungry people in Ueno Park. He ate no dinner, saved no money for himself and carried the milk kettles two miles back to the center so he wouldn't have to pay taxi fare.

Next morning he expressed the concern he had for these destitute people. In broken English he said, "Ueno people very hungry. I am lucky boy." We have never felt anyone display so much genuine thankfulness for benefits received and so much passion for fellowmen.

We asked Shiba-san later why he spent his money in this way instead of buying a shirt or something for himself. He said, "As you know I spoke several times to the poor people at Ueno about God's love for them. When you gave me the money I thought that I would now have an opportunity to *show* them that God loves them. They needed the food more than I needed a shirt."

Whoever shares with others should do it generously; whoever shows kindness to others should do it cheerfully. Love must be completely sincere. Share your belongings with your needy fellow Christians, and open your homes to strangers.

-Romans 12:8, 9, 13; The Good News Bible-

PANORAMA

"Seventeen hundred air-conditioned rooms, four dining rooms, three cocktail lounges" -- so reads the description on the picture postcard showing the Chase-Park Plaza Hotel in St. Louis, Missouri.

Today I sat long in its lobby and watched the shuttling, shuffling scene, ate in the cheapest of its dining rooms, and scanned the 392 pages of the *Sunday Post-Dispatch*. I sat and looked and listened and read with no duties pressing, waiting for the opening of the thirtieth anniversary convention of the National Association of Evangelicals.

And as I sat, I became startlingly aware of the incredibly heightened standard of today's living. My amazement nearly matched that of eight years ago when my wife and I returned from twelve years of relief work overseas. The contrast then of coming from one of the poorest of the Third World nations into the richest of countries was sharp, but not much more sharp than today's awareness of the astonishing *increase* of affluent living in already richest America during the intervening years since our return.

The 'deluxeness' of the hotel facilities; the costly, high quality clothing; the preponderance of luxury items in newspaper and magazine advertising and the profligacy of the advertising; the diamonds; the Cadillacs; the casualness of big spending -- it all adds up to a self-satisfying binge of materialism with unconscionable waste and discards! I did not know I was poor until I saw the proffered salaries in the classified section of the newspaper.

I,too, I find, respond to luxury. I like life smooth. The longer I'm back from Africa, the more easily I can salve my conscience in buying big dinners and big ties, even though I know my good and intelligent Christian friend, Gregory Nzungize, is starving. Surrounded by plenty, I think of him less often.

I read an article in today's *Parade Magazine* by Lloyd Shearer, in which he quotes Dwight Eisenhower regarding arms expenditures in 1953: "Every gun that is made," Eisenhower declared, "every warship launched, every rocket fired signifies, in the final sense, a theft from those who hunger and are not fed, those who are cold and are not clothed." And he concluded, "This is not a way of life at all. Under the cloud of war, it is humanity hanging from a cross of iron."

And I thought as I saw the affluence all around me today, someone is being robbed of the necessities of life so that we can have the luxuries of life. And I wondered further whether, if Christ were in the lobby throng today, He would be conformed to the prevailing elegant dress and nine dollar broad, bright tie?

I wondered more. Would He eat our ten-dollar dinners and tenant our thirty-five dollar rooms? I do not know for sure. But I do know that since He is omniscient and all-loving, He would be much more aware than are we of the multiplied millions who are hungry for food and love and whom He loves as much as He does us.

If I have made gold my hope or have said to the fine gold, thou art my confidence; if I have rejoiced because my wealth was great and because mine hand had gotten much, this would have been an iniquity for I should have denied the God that is above.

-Job 31:25, 28; The King James Version-

PHOTOS DO NOT TELL ALL

Emaciated mothers and ragged children usually make the best photo subjects for the publicity department of a relief organization. Hong Kong is a happy hunting ground for a photographer bent on collecting pathetic-looking subjects. Indeed, not long ago, in a tenement house where refugee families rent bed spaces, we ourselves came across a sunken-eyed, skinny child which matches any publicity brochure picture we've ever seen.

We, too, have occasionally sent such "sympathy-provoking" photos to our organization headquarters office. The pictures were not faked; our home folks need to see some of the tragic conditions as they exist in the world.

But we also periodically submit for publication some "brighter" photos, the kind which do not give dramatic impressions of poverty. The happy smiling faces of refugee children at one of our Christmas bundle distributions on a resettlement house rooftop is one included in our "brighter" photo file.

The brighter photo needs to be interpreted; it does not tell all. These, we know, have a double meaning. Whereas the meaning of a pathetic photo is easy to interpret, only those who know the tragic backgrounds of the families from which the smiling children come can identify what they see in the brighter photo. They know that the smiles and the cleaner-than-could-be-expected clothing are the reflections of the resilient and stoical character of the parents. The children have learned from their parents how to smile through tears.

The mother of such a family washes and charcoal irons her boy's only shirt at night so that it will be fresh to wear in the morning. Such a mother deserves to be helped as much as does the discouraged mother who lets the boy and his shirt get dirtier with the days until the boy is a fit subject for the tragic type of photo.

Need does not always go begging; it is not always plain to see. And need that hides and smiles calls for admiration on top of sympathy. The photo of a ragged beggar with his pathetic penury poses may cause immediate reactions. Some concern, however, should be reserved for the mother who smiles and silently suffers while her children are experiencing unknown fates in mainland China.

We cannot stop lifting the deadweight from those who are down. But let us not neglect to offer helping hands to those who gamely bounce back from their year to year bouts with destitution. Courage needs encouragement as much as does discouragement.

I have learned to be satisfied with what I have. I know what it is to be in need and what it is to have more than enough. I have learned this secret, so that anywhere, at any time, I am content, whether I am full or hungry, whether I have too much or too little. I have strength to face all conditions by the power that Christ gives me.

-Philippians 4:11-13, The Good News Bible-

GETTING USED TO PLENTY

The Roy Bakers, longtime missionaries in India, have been having notable results in film evangelism. I met them at a rescue mission in Chicago where they purchased the 16-millimeter Bolex movie camera which I had used in my round-the-world photographic mission for MCC in 1960. The Bakers had just returned on furlough and were supplementing their movie equipment. Mrs. Baker expressed a problem in adjustment they were experiencing since their arrival in the States. She wrote in a letter:

"We are having trouble to adjust to an entirely different environment and way of life. I pray that you will be grateful every day for this country in which you live. I cannot begin to describe the poverty and misery and sadness of millions of people in the land of India. There are hundreds of thousands who do not have the things that the people here throw away. What a joy it is to turn on the taps and get hot water, or any kind of water for that matter, and to see lovely fine white sugar and to use flour with no weevils in it, and to buy cottage cheese and so many goodies that we haven't been able to have for years! Do pray for us that the love of Christ will constrain us to return to India joyfully."

A PARABLE OF INTERNATIONAL FRIENDSHIP

And it came to pass that a plane from over the Pacific did bear on its silver wings to San Francisco's Golden Gate forty-two sons and daughters of the Land of the Rising Sun.

Now it was so that this was not an ordinary air safari. For notwithstanding their awareness of the Hiroshima tragedy, these new-generation Japanese youth were bent on a mission of goodwill to the very land where that thing, the bomb, had been made. They intended the flight should span, not only the Pacific's expanse of water, but also the chasm of international misunderstandings and difference and customs.

But verily, few could fly, like they, this mission of peace. A bridge must be built, they said, a bridge of friendship and understanding over which millions now separated and estranged may come and go and learn to love one another.

And it came to pass that no sooner did they land early on a Sunday morning than the goodwill emissaries addressed themselves to the task of building a bridgehead. They photographed everything they saw. And from that moment onward did they diligently endeavor to see and experience. The bridgehead had to have a firm base of understanding.

And, behold, when the American hosts saw how eager the guests from the Orient were to understand the West, they lost no time in coming alongside them in the common task of building the bridgehead. And in the following four weeks a lot of debris was cleared away (suspicions, prejudices, misunderstandings) and many building blocks of experience were hewn out of both Japanese and American quarries and firmly cemented together with the mixture of Eastern and Western kindness.

Behold some of the building blocks that were mined: colorful stones of Sequoia and Yosemite natural beauty; rare rocks of Japanese grace and culture; slabs of American agricultural and industrial scientific achievements; highly polished marble from the universities of both countries; foursquare crystal cubes mined in Christian homes; Rock of Ages granite from the churches -- these and many more like them were the experience blocks of enduring stone that went into the building of the bridgehead.

Verily, verily the bridgehead was built well, for when the time of parting came, behold, they wept, both guests and hosts!

And when the guests were leaving the Golden Gate of the West to return to their Land of the Rising Sun, they looked down and saw the bridgehead, beautiful and firm, lifting its arms up and over the water, ready for a second span.

Now from the observation plaza of the airport, the American hosts were watching the plane melt away into the blue Pacific haze, thinking back on the unusual events of the four weeks just ended, and thinking forward to the day when they, too, would be swallowed up by the same Pacific space.

For behold, they had accepted the invitation to help build the bridgehead on the other side.

WHY?

Although the MCC mass distributions of food, clothing and medicines in Japan were not as large as were post-war distributions in Germany and Austria, the Christian witness of our relief effort in the Island Kingdom was possibly more telling, coming as it did so soon after Japan's capitulation. A simple milk-serving project in Tokyo illustrates the point:

The city's labor department located in downtown Tokyo designated certain locations throughout the city where the unemployed could come mornings for assignment to a day's work. With several helpers we mixed milk powder and served cups of hot milk at two of these locations where several thousand men and women assembled daily, many of them without breakfast.

The project ran several months until one day newspaper reporters with a camera crew, both still and movie, appeared on the scene to film the simple operation of milk-serving and the presentation of a certificate of appreciation by officials of the Tokyo Labor Department. Three metropolitan newspapers carried the story the following morning, and several days later MCC personnel were interviewed on television as to *why* we Americans, Japan's erstwhile enemies, were returning to perform this social service. Thus an opportunity was provided to give a Christian witness over news media that covered a good part of the country, and this where only one half of one per cent of the people is Christian!

UNGRATEFULNESS IN DISTRIBUTIONS

When a relief worker brings food and clothing to Africans and Indians or Chinese, he is sometimes taken aback by their seeming ungratefulness for the gifts which the Christians of the West send to them. He meets up with a take-it-for-granted attitude which he did not expect. Not too infrequently the recipients argue for more and better things than what is given them. This realistic state of things comes as quite a shock to the new relief worker who had expected that the dark faces of these underprivileged masses would be wreathed in smiles when the cornmeal and used clothing were handed out to them.

Many of them are, let it be said. In more than a dozen years of relief work overseas, we have seen a million smiles and heard thousands of thank-you's in different languages. We have seen tears of sincere gratitude. The letters and the tokens of appreciation which they sometimes give in return do warm the heart of the relief worker.

But the fact remains that there are other than smiling faces in the mass distribution lines: expressionless faces, stolid faces, tired faces, even faces that register anger and ill will.

To explain this phenomenon of relief distributing, it must be kept in mind how deep and wide is the chasm that separates the few of us who have the good things in life from the masses of them who don't, and that in these modern days of facilitated communication, they are seeing what we have. And true to human nature, they want what we have; they feel that what we give them is only a little of what is due them.

In case this phenomenon should deter constituent giving, let it be said that in only one year in post-war Germany we received 2500 thank-you letters, and more than once did refugees kiss our hands out of heartfelt gratefulness. Relief effort *has* been worthwhile.

ARE WE CLIQUISH?
(Written in 1970 after Round-the World Evaluation Trip)

In this world of four billion people are multiplied thousands of little and bigger groups: circles, neighborhoods, families, societies, communities, cliques.

Each one of these groups of human beings has its own concerns and limits. For the members of each group, their group is their "world." They are unaware, or vaguely so, of other groups. The Pygmy tribespeople of Central Africa are unaware of that group of men called the Reedley City Council and its problems, just as the members of the Reedley First Mennonite Church are unaware of the city of shack-dwellers in the marshy waterfront of Bombay, India. For each group, most of the other groups do not exist. Each has its own concerns, and frankly, does not want to know too much about and identify with the problems and the troubles of "outside" and far-away groups with their strange ways of thinking and doing.

As I come back to what has been my "world" for five years at the Reedley Clothing Center, following a two-months trip around the world, I am a bit more aware of my world citizenship and the responsibilities which this citizenship entails.

On a boundless imaginary screen I am projecting, as I write, the simultaneous doings of the countless groups I touched on this trip, and as I watch this spectacle, the importance of the groups of which I am a member become deflated, and I am myself cut down to size. I am one of many and God has no pets.

Satan, the enemy of mankind, has done a stupendous job in getting individuals and groups to pit their own egoistic interests against those of others. Here lies the basic cause of world troubles, and this trip has made me more aware of the exceeding cunning of this common Enemy of Mankind. Scripture enjoins us Christians to look not only on our own things, but also on the things of others, and the look-in which this trip has afforded has increased my compassion for people in the sorry and tragic messes Satan has tricked them into.

There are other impressions which I have received from this trip which I would like to write about: the increasing difficulties for MCC fieldmen in getting relief goods through to the bottom people who really need it; the very commendable self-giving of our area directors under these difficulties; the trend in MCC relief work in giving a (personal) hand instead of just a handout; the fact that everywhere the rich seem to be getting richer, the poor poorer.

But to keep within space bounds, I mean to emphasize here that we enlarge our sympathy and understanding of those outside our own groups, that we jag the Big-I windbag, and that we render our supreme allegiance to Christ who has been the only One able to outwit the cunning of the Archenemy of Mankind.

I would challenge us to be less group-cliquish, to open our eyes, to raise our sights and to play a bigger role in the *total* Kingdom of God through Jesus Christ our Lord.

For when you have become full and prosperous and have built fine homes to live in, and when your flocks and herds have become very large, and your silver and gold have multiplied, that is the time to watch out that you don't become proud, and forget the Lord your God who brought you out of your slavery in the land of Egypt.

-Deuteronomy 8:12-14, The Living Bible-

DOESN'T ANYONE CARE?

The newspaper reporter was on his beat. It was nearly midnight. From a rooftop came the crying of a woman. He climbed the stairway to where refugee shacks made an additional inhabited "floor" of the flat roof of the building. In one of the makeshift shacks the reporter found the crying woman.

She was a Chinese woman, a flesh-and-blood human being in Hong Kong of whom you and I and nearly everyone else in the world had been unaware. Huddled around her were five children and a sixth was soon to be born. The children's ages were twelve, ten, five, four and three.

The reason for her crying was that several days before, her husband, a very good husband, had died, and the children were hungry, and there was no one now to earn money. Not only did she not have money, but she was also owing for medical treatment her husband had had before he died.

The heart of the newspaper reporter was touched, and when a roving reporter in refugee-packed Hong Kong singles out for publication one of the many tragic cases he meets with, one can know that the situation is indeed a desperate one.

The morning paper carried the story. The father, the article said, himself born into a poor family, and the mother, an orphan, had married in China and had come to Hong Kong like so many other refugees with the high hopes of bettering their lot. But in the fierce competition that is Hong Kong, the years brought strings of reverses that eventuated in the rooftop scene the reporter was describing. Not one of the children had ever gone to school; how could the children go when there was not enough to eat! Was there not someone somewhere, the article concluded, who would come to the rescue of this pregnant, just-widowed woman and her children?

Loretta Lau, our Chinese MCC co-worker, caught the item in her Chinese language newspaper. "Should we do something about it?" she asked when she came to the office that morning. It was agreed that, although there would no doubt be many others responding with help, MCC investigate the case.

When the MCC workers found the rooftop and the woman and the children, they knew the reporter had not exaggerated. More details came to light. When the father died, the refugee neighbors pooled from five to twenty cents each to buy a burying box. A dozen rooftop families were also pooling food, each family one spoonful from its own meager fare. But the neighbors could not continue sharing, and the baby was due in a few days, and what would happen when the mother would be away having the baby?

The big surprise of the visit was that no one else had come in response to the reporter's plea. No one seemed to care.

The MCC team pitched in. They brought food and vitamins, they outfitted the children and the mother with fresh clothing, and readied a layette for the expected baby. Loretta spoke words of comfort to the mother and later visited her in the charity hospital. The older children were encouraged to mother the younger. And when the mother brought back her baby to the fatherless rooftop brood, MCC continued supplying them with food.

"Christians must be good people," one of the rooftop neighbors remarked.

But how little MCC's help was! With mass distribution and school-feeding projects requiring major attention, there was little time for MCC personnel to devote to individual cases. MCC's food and clothing and Christmas bundles were indeed help in a critical need, but basically the status of the fatherless family remained tragically the same: a widow with six children, living in a packing box on the roof of a tenement house; no breadwinner, no income, and no prospect for bettering their situation.

Would that there had been someone to give himself to this family, to get under the load, to share, to care! Were one of our luxury-satiated American Christians to give unstintingly of self and silver to this bedraggled family, what unguessed springs of joy would be discovered! The adventurer for God and fellowmen (going beyond even the duty of the Peace Corpsman) assuredly has heavy loads and rocky roads, but when he is doing it for others, the way seems easy and the burden light. The Chinese widow needed someone to weep with her, and then -- to rejoice with her.

It seems to me we Christians (including myself) are much too much self-oriented, egocentric. We do not "look upon the things of others." We lack the imagination to project ourselves into the lives of suffering fellowmen. And there are a billion people in the world who, like the Chinese refugee widow, have heavy loads and rocky roads!

Let us be challenged by God Himself through the prophet Isaiah (58:6-8): "Is not this the fast that I have chosen? to loose the bands of wickedness, to undo the heavy burdens, and to let the oppressed go free, and that ye break every yoke? Is it not to deal thy bread to the hungry, and that thou bring the poor that are cast out to thy house? When thou seest the naked that thou cover him; and that thou hide not thyself from thine own flesh? *Then* shall thy light break forth as the morning, and thine health shall spring forth speedily; and thy righteousness shall go before thee; the glory of the Lord shall be thy reward."

(NOTE: The children mentioned in the above story appear in the color sound film, "Hong Kong Report." They were filmed in an MCC distribution scene during the time the mother was in hospital giving birth to the sixth child. The 18-minute film is available from the office of Information Services, Mennonite Central Committee, Akron, PA 17501.)

What God the Father considers to be pure and genuine religion is this: to take care of orphans and widows in their suffering and to keep himself from being corrupted by the world.

-James 1:27, The Good News Bible-

GERHARD NEUFELDT

Last Monday I brought Gerhard Neufeldt, 72, from Neuminster to Hamburg in one of Hitler's famous Volkswagens, and as we drove the 75 kilometers he told me that he had taught school for thirty years in Russia; that he had been imprisoned and sentenced to be shot for his faith in Christ; that in a deliverance no less miraculous than the Apostle Paul's, he escaped the firing squad; that his brother-in-law died of starvation in Siberia; that his two sons are still in Siberia; that he and his wife and his two daughters have been displaced and re-displaced in their flight westward, finally landing in Neuminster in the British Zone of Germany; and that the Russians tricked a close friend of his into giving them the address of the miserable little hovel he and his wife have been occupying in Neuminster. Now he must move again ("You don't know the Russians," he said) and go into hiding in another town, and I witnessed the parting of this aged Brother (I say "Brother" for he put his arms around me and kissed me out of sheer joy of Christian friendship) from his malnutritioned wife, not knowing when they would meet again.

One statement he made will always remain with me. After recounting how the glory of heaven and the presence of the Lord filled the execution chamber during the two days he was its occupant, and how oblivious he was of his emaciated condition, the lice, the vermin, the stink and even of his imminent death, he made the following statement: "Theological and Bible Students believe God is and that the Bible is true. They believe, but I KNOW."

II

MENNONITE CENTRAL COMMITTEE

MCC MUST BE FELT

I had an occasion recently to spend three weeks in the headquarters office of the Mennonite Central Committee. Although I've been directly or indirectly related to MCC for a quarter century, this was the first I'd had an assigned desk in the main office.

I never could explain just what MCC is. I still can't, even after three weeks in the head office.

One does not explain MCC. One *feels* MCC.

I felt it as I sat there those three weeks surrounded by the area directors at their desks and the secretaries at their typewriters.

Here was MCC's nerve center. Communications were flowing between the center and half a thousand MCC-labeled people in the nearer and farther reaches of the world.

In voices which only the microphones in their hands heard, administrators were dictating their recommendations and encouragements to field workers, and across the aisle, secretaries were tapping out the letters, some of which would inevitably be destiny-determining.

I sensed the drama of it: roles being played out here that would bring life and joy to millions; pulsations from MCC's heart that were being felt by needy people everywhere.

How MCC personnel, with the usual complements of human frailties and with varying shades of Christian faith, can unite in a worldwide ministry of compassion, and do it without fanfare as I have observed it at Akron, this is a miracle that God has wrought, and that is why it is hard for me to describe MCC. MCC is more an organism than it is an organization.

I could write a sizable book on what is wrong with MCC. But in spite of what I think is wrong, and what others think is wrong, God has unmistakably used this His instrument, so that today literally multi-millions of people around the world know the name MCC in many languages -- including the language of love -- and thank God for it.

So MCC moves on. My three-week sensing of the heart and mind of MCC as an observer confirms the conviction I had as an activist that MCC is of God. I was much impressed with the quiet assumption of duties at hand, with the Christian protocol so plain to see, with the spirit of youth in the midst, with the all-around increased efficiencies, and with the dedication of the personnel from veteran administrators to youngbloods. God *is* in MCC!

And that is why I cannot explain MCC.

I was eyes to the blind, and feet was I to the lame. I was a father to the poor.
-Job 29:15, 16; The King James Version-

THE TWO

(Written on the occasion of the Fiftieth Anniversary of MCC. Orie O. Miller and Clayton Kratz were the first MCC workers.)

Out of the West they came,
The Two.
They saw and felt
they multiplied themselves
and came again.
and again
by sea
by train
by plane.
They shared the pain
of wars:
War I
War II

They went home
but they could not rest.

For now that eyes
had learned to see
and hearts to pain,
they added
darkskins
to their list of brothers.

They came again,
they got themselves
mixed up
with the masses
in the festering East,
and along the Congo
and Amazon morasses
and e'en in prostrate Haiti.

They wept
at sight and plight
of fellowmen--
and stayed.

Yesterday
hate exploded
at home.
The shock
sent youth
to city ghettos,
to Appalachia.

And now
at end of fifty years
the extended arms of
The Two
enfold the needy
of the world,
both far and near.

It must continue so.
The world is sick.
Never
has it needed
more desperately
Christian compassion.
Never
have we needed to love
more genuinely
the sick,
the distraught of earth.

OUT OF THE FIRES

A Poem written for the First Dinner Meeting
of all West Coast MCC-Related Committees.
12/5/69

Out of the fires of persecution,
Sufferings dire, and prosecution,
Was born in empathy and pity
The Mennonite Central Committee.

Handmaid of the church, she first did aid
The brethren, but then did escalade
Her Christian conscience to too include
Anyone with great necessitude.

Her roots imbedded deep in ground
Of pietistic faith profound,
She thus did add a new dimension
By her min'stries of compassion.

Her name now came to a million ears
In fifty lands, o'er fifty years,
She shares today the heavy loads
Of countless men on Jericho Roads.

Is't now too much, these heavy loads?
Shall we withdraw t'affluent abodes,
Draw in turtle-like, be less involved?
The MCC vision dissolve?

SHEDDING ABROAD GOD'S LOVE

The words of the Apostle Paul in his letter to the Thessalonians (chapter 5, verse 5) carry a depth of meaning which may be missed in a casual reading. He speaks of the love of God as being *shed abroad* in one's heart. When we shed tears, the eyes are suffused in the waters of emotion. It is something like this that takes place in our hearts; the heart is bathed in love.

For Christians who have experienced the overwhelming love of God, it is natural for them, in turn, is it not, to *shed abroad* the same love. As roses shed their perfume on the air about them, so we should send forth our love and concern to people both near and far away. The dictionary definition for "abroad" is: "far and wide," "beyond narrow limits," "beyond the bounds of one's home grounds."

Now I like to think of MCC as a *shedding abroad* organization. Many people know Akron as a sending abroad place, a place from which go out many tons of relief goods to needy people overseas. But there is a difference between sending abroad and shedding abroad. Sending abroad can be mechanical and without perfume. Shedding abroad, on the other hand, involves the heart. Love and prayers and sincere concern go with the relief goods. There is an empathy that does not forget when the gift is given and the ship pulls away from the New York and San Francisco piers. The donor goes along with his gift.

In our deputation visits to many hundreds of churches in the United States and Canada, Eunice and I have noted this warmness of heart, this love fragrance in the giving of MCC's constituency, and we have felt the response to this love in our distributions overseas. In a distribution to 1,300 refugee families in Kiel, Germany in 1948, the German man who was helping me to open the bales of blankets and clothing, gazed for a long time at the quilts as they rolled out and exclaimed, "Wie viel Liebe!" ("How much love!")

"As touching brotherly love," says Paul in 1 Thes. 4:9 and 10 (NEV), "we appeal to you, brothers, to do better still." Certainly in these evil days that have come upon the world MCCers need to go and shed as well as send God's love!

A RAGPICKER'S LETTER

(Written after his first time at MCC Center. Translated by Mana Horikawa)

Dear MCC People:

I thank God and you from the bottom of my heart for that I was given an opportunity to visit you. How long have I not experienced such a warm, homely atmosphere that I have dreamed. Of course I appreciated those delicious dishes and tea very much, but more than all I was so impressed by your "eyes" full of goodwill and love. They made my stubborn heart warmed as if the spring sun would melt the snow heaped during the long winter. The memory of that joyous afternoon we had together at Tamagawa, singing hymns and talking nicely, will encourage me through the rest of my life.

For the last many years we have had to endure all those inhuman treatments. And we have almost forgotten human feeling -- anger, resistance and even sorrow. Sometimes we have met some nice people who showed kindness to us, but we could not trust them, for we thought they did all those things to us only by their curiosity.

It was last October that I was invited by you for the first time. Although I wanted to visit you right away, something made me hesitate and I refused your invitation. But at the same time I felt something made my heart ache; I regretted my attitude whenever I recalled your warm and kind smiles. You can understand how happy I was then when I visited your place last Sunday.

My parents passed away and I have no relatives. I have been so lonesome for a long time. But now I feel I saw God through your innocent, warm smiles.

III

MISCELLANEOUS

IT SEEMS TO ME

Although he thought
the matter ought
to be *that way,*
it seems to me
that it should be
this way!

An argument abrewing here?

Not necessarily.

There are many differences of opinion that are not fought over. More often than we realize, we humans agree to disagree. We could not get along together otherwise.

There are, of course, social and spiritual fundamentals we all must concur on if we are to live in this world and gain Heaven in the world to come. But beyond the basics are the fields of interpretation and opinion where Christians respect each other's viewpoint. There must be the emphatic *"I know!"* indeed. But there must likewise be the less assertive "It seems to me."

Who among us has not experienced deep and unshakable convictions! And who, too, has not learned how unstable and volatile our more shallow ideas, views and opinions can be! What seemed important to us ten years ago seems no longer so. On the other hand, what seemed incidental during our youth may have become central in later years. We change with the passing of time and the gaining of experience.

One way to gain experience fast is to live in a foreign land. Twelve years of relief work in five different countries with their differing cultures have resulted in a great many shiftings of emphasis and opinion for Eunice and me. Some of our thinking has moved toward the center and opinions have moved outward toward the circumference. We can never be the same because of what we have heard and seen and experienced.

Many of our home friends ask us, "How does it seem to be back home?" In other words, they are asking what Americans and Brethren in Christ and relatives look like in the setting of the wider perspective.

We hasten to reply that we are still Americans and that we have no less love and respect for our home friends than before we went away. But we must add that while we grasp the hands of friends here with warmth and appreciation, we also cannot forget the far-off friends whom we lately bade goodbye. We accept with unfeigned thanks the outpourings of love and hospitality from our homefolks, but we cannot chase from the other side of the laden dinner table the ghost of the Chinese refugee with the empty rice bowl. The hungry and the needy have come along home with us.

Since we have returned from service overseas we have been sharing some of our impressions and convictions, and the statement of them may sometimes hurt. On the other hand, where interpretations and opinions are involved, I try to preface them generously with "It seems to me," for I well know that in peripheral issues what may seem to me to be *this way* may seem to you the reader to be *that way*, and both of us being human, each has equal right to his interpretation or opinion. Above all, may the Lord keep me from giving the impression that I have all the answers. I am still in the primary school, or so it seems to me.

LETTER TO HANDEL

(In Response to *TIME's* "God is Dead" Issue)

I was listening to your oratorio, Handel, on Easter Sunday when, in the middle of the "Hallelujah Chorus," my eyes fell on *TIME's* three blood-red words. With a pang and the bang of a rubber balloon, my soul crashed. Why did you do it, Handel? Why did you perpetrate this hoax on us? Why did you perpetrate a god-myth? Now whom will kings and commoners stand up for? Your "Hallelujah Chorus" becomes now a hollowlujah chorus, uninspired and uninspiring, for the learned ones did declare that God is dead. Why did you do it, Handel? Why did you raise our hopes so high, only for them to be dashed to the ground, now that the truth is known?

P.S.: But you certainly did a good job at convincing us that "Messiah" was going to live forever and ever!

AFTER

To be weak, after being strong; to find one's self surpassed after being in authority in a particular field; to be poor after being rich; to see the wrinkles come after gaining Hollywood stardom; to be ignored after heading the group; to be wheel-chaired after the accident -- these are facts in human living that are often hard to accept.

For irreconcilables, unadaptables, and self-aggrandizers, these lessons are learned bitterly. "It can't be!" exclaims one. "I won't!" shouts another. For them life takes on the proportions of tragedy.

Better is the expectation and the acceptance of facts. To accept gracefully and courageously the changes that come to all, even death itself, can turn tragedy into victory.

Many times Jesus said, "My hour is not yet come," but when His hour did come, He met it bravely. Loss of power, position and health brings a compensating peace and satisfaction when faced in the spirit of Christ.

THINNING OUT

Hair and old friends thin out with age.

So many of our old friends have slipped away, even in the past twelve months. Year after year we've been stroking out the names of lifelong friends from the mailing list for our Season's Greetings. Suddenly we become aware of how few are left. Eunice and I find ourselves surprised we're still around.

It makes us feel a little lonely.

One generation does not communicate with the next from the grave. The now generation doesn't *know* the neighborhood and family atmospheres, the social and spiritual mores of yesterday. It seems there isn't a common meeting ground between old and young in our now generation.

Adding to this loneliness is the change in the world itself. What was once wrong is now right and right is wrong; black is white and white black, and all the shades of grey between but serve to heighten the feeling of strangeness of today's world. That we are pilgrims and strangers becomes ever more evident.

This experience of course is not new. Some generations back, Shakespeare put it well. "The times," he said of his own day, "are out of joint." And the Children of Israel complained that life in the desert was not what it used to be when they had leeks and onions to eat in Egypt.

For better or for worse, the fact of change is universal and irrevocable.

NONAGENARIANS

Through our travels in the various states, Eunice and I have come to know some remarkable very old people who are a joy and a challenge to us younger oldsters. We'd like to share the inspiration of seven of them, all of whom are over ninety.

Of these nonagenarians, one is a gentleman, four are mothers of many progeny, and two are belles that have never been rung. Four of them live in California, one in Arizona, one in Pennsylvania and one in Wisconsin. All are unusually well preserved in body and mind and show a common trait of wanting to do for themselves. Five of these still live alone, doing housekeeping. Some quilt and garden and walk unaided to post office and church. Two of them still drive cars, providing taxi service for younger older folk.

The Pennsylvanian is the youngest looking and can be taken for twenty years below her real age. She is active and alert in situations at home and at her church. One of the two maiden ladies has just returned from a tour to the Holy Land, while the other is still active in prison evangelism. The "gentleman" is so designated purposely, for his outstanding trait of character is his optimism, his thoughtfulness of others and his chivalry, a man of the "old school" who rises when ladies enter the room. He never complains, doesn't wear glasses, says he doesn't have an ache or a pain. He recently renewed his covenant with God, bought a big and a little Bible, and reads them both.

The Arizonan spent a lifetime of mission work in China, and so enthusiastic in the work of the Lord has she remained that only last year she wrote three hundred Christmas letters by hand, receiving and absorbing a commensurate number of replies. Her letters are paeans of rejoicing and thanksgiving in the Lord. The unmarried lady who is active in prison evangelism just turned ninety-six, lives in Wisconsin, and is the only one of the seven whom we have not met personally.

Except the Pennsylvanian, all of these have had the experience of trekking westward as pioneers, some of them by covered wagon. Besides the rigors of travel, there stretched out the years of getting their roots down into the soil. So much a lifestyle has hard labor become for these brave souls that it is natural for them to want to continue their industrious ways into the evening of life. Being

Christians, they have not developed the profligate wastings of energy and resources so common to the younger generation of today.

It is interesting how we became acquainted with the 96-year-old lady from Wisconsin. She had come into possession of my two books of conversion stories entitled, "I Was Born Again" and "Twice Born," and wrote to enquire where the books might be purchased in quantity. "It surely hurts me that your books are no longer in print," she wrote, "and how I wish I had stocked up on these while they were still on the bookshelves."

I replied that I had a few copies still on hand and quoted a special quantity price. Back came her order for thirty copies of each title. I sent the books and in an accompanying letter asked if she would tell me more about herself. I would like to convey to my readers the spirit of this remarkable woman by quoting almost verbatim the long letter which she sent in response:

"Dear Brother Wingert:

"You ask me to tell you more about myself. What should I say? I was born at Broadhead, Wisconsin on July 20, 1883, which will make me 96 if I live to July (1979). I live alone and keep my house. Occasionally I walk the half mile to the Post Office and to church. I have not been very well the past year but I realize I have much more for which to thank God than most people have.

"We moved West a little before I was three years old. I was the only girl of seven children. Out west we could not go to school. It was too far and there were dangerous blizzards. We could not even go to church. But whenever Mother sat down to nurse a baby, I insisted on bringing her the Bible so she could read to me. Our distant neighbors were Bohemians, and we could not understand them. I had to be a second mother, diapering babies when I was only six while Mother was working in the field. We never had toys that were bought in the stores. We played with buffalo bones found on the prairies and with hen's feathers, building fences and finding white lambs in the sky. We had each other and were happier than any pampered child I ever knew.

"Besides, Mother told us Bible stories, read to us and talked to us about the Lord Jesus until I lost my heart to Him. I said my prayers at Mother's knee when I was very young. I can see myself when not yet four standing at her knee, learning 'Thou God seest me.' Soon the verse saved the day in temptation.

"I truly think I had a rich childhood. When I was eleven we moved to Broadhead again where I entered school, attended Sunday School and preaching. I gave my first testimony, shy as I was, when I was nearly twelve. Though before a big audience, I just had to rise and announce, 'I love the Lord.' That night as I knelt beside my bed, heaven came down to earth. There are things that cannot be described. No one ever told me I had to read the Bible, but from then on I never thought of such a thing as letting a day pass without spending time with it. I loved it, although my lack of schooling made reading hard and slow.

"I never ran the streets as children do, but rushed home to care for my young brothers, wash dishes, do what was needed. I never knew I was abused. The babies were my dolls. I loved them.

"We were very poor. Most moderns would never believe the privations we went through. When we were all down sick one winter, my mother was up all night, even though she believed she was coming down with pneumonia. The floor had big cracks, letting in the bitter cold. We were far from neighbors, Mother was a widow, and there was no way of obtaining food. And we were all out of food. Mother said she told God, 'Here is Your chance to prove that Your Word is true.' Think of the testing she went through when she had to wait till near noon with seven children before God sent help. A woman down the street, not knowing there was need, had been baking for the week and cooking all kinds of food such as we never had seen before, when an emergency called her out of town. She had to dispose of all that food and remembered where there was a family of children. Did our eyes bulge out!

"Later when I was in high school I was wearing shoes in desperate shape. On the way to school I said to the Lord, 'I am Your child, but I am no advertisement to You.' I had gone only two blocks when a woman met me at her door with a pair of shoes in her hand. She said, 'I can't wear these. Perhaps you can.' This should be enough to show that God mercifully gave me a wholesome start in life.

"I am making this letter too long, but I will say that God's mercies have continued all my days. I taught school for many years -- country school, grade school and high school. I started out at $25 a month and got only $30 to $35 a month for years, and I was the family's main support. I never got much, for it was just before salaries started to rise. I had to go home to care for Mother. In the depression I washed windows for ten cents an hour. I do not feel abused in the least. Today I live on a small social security check, have learned to conserve, have never had a chance to develop expensive tastes nor desire to swim in high society.

"God gives me in my old age some joy when old pupils write, 'You were our only Christian teacher and you helped me so much.' We could talk about the Savior right in the class in those days. I used to become so burdened for those young people.

"I got my education a little at a time and have a Master's degree. You would never believe how little my food cost me.

"My maternal grandfather was a preacher in the mid-1800's in the then wilds of Minnesota, who never in his life asked for a penny from anyone nor lived on a salary. He thought that if God sent him to tell people the Way of Salvation, God would support him. My oldest brother spent years preaching in the West in schoolhouses all over the country three times every Sunday in three different places and again on Sunday evening. A second brother who preached all his life died this winter at the age of 90. I have two grandnephews preaching now.

"How I love God's Word! I have often sat down with The Book at 8 a.m. and found myself there yet at 2 p.m., forgetful of dinner. I know if I lived many lifetimes I would just begin to get what is in that wonderful Book.

"I have never written a letter like this to a stranger. But I felt you were a brother. And the Great Day is coming when we shall no longer be strangers. In HIM we love, (s) B. M. B."

POMP

A fifty-foot strip of red carpet was being unrolled to the door of the first class passenger cabin as we, the "common herd," were entering the large economy-fare compartment of the China (Nationalist) Air Lines plane. The flight was to be from Seoul, Korea to Taipei, Taiwan. a 26-man military honor guard in spotless white uniforms then took precise position along the edges of the unrolled and newly swept plush walkway.

For half an hour the guard stood at attention, while inside for half an hour we waited and gawked, wondering who the august personage would be who was being accorded the special honor. He must be very VIP, for only for such would the airline delay its scheduled flight, using up fifty hours of passenger time.

Four limousines finally rolled onto the airport pad. Out came a dozen non-uniformed men. The tallest of them and a second man were surrounded by a battery of cameras. They were evidently guest and host of an important state affair.

After posings and hand-shakings and bowings, the smiling but dignified principals stepped onto the red carpet, the host going only part way, the guest walking the full length of the red carpet and casually mounting the steps to his first class seat. A few minutes more and the craft was airborne.

As we were sailing across the China Sea, I thought I saw a tiny bit of history made; I was seeing the most recent of the long list of VIP's of the Ancient East's forty-century history -- kings, knights and conquerors who have come and gone. I reflected long on the pomp and foibles of men, and on life.

Said Shakespeare, "All the world's a stage, and all the men and women merely players; each has his entrance and his exit." And the Psalmist says men are like grass that grows up and flourishes in the morning, and is cut down and withers in the evening.

P.S.: This evening's paper headlines the visit of Brigadier General Srey Samane to Korea and his coming talks with the Nationalist Chinese government tomorrow. He is personal and special envoy of Cambodian Prime Minister Lon Nol for the establishment of diplomatic relations between Cambodia and Nationalist China. The

Chinese government has decide in principle to extend aid to the anti-Communist government of Lon Nol who ousted Prince Sihanouk in a coup last March 18 while Sihanouk was in Moscow. .

Remember that there will be difficult times in the last days. People will be selfish, greedy, boastful, and conceited; they will be insulting, disobedient to their parents, ungrateful, and irreligious; they will be unkind, merciless, slanderers, violent, and fierce; they will hate the good; they will be treacherous, reckless, and swollen with pride; they will love pleasure rather than God; they will hold to the outward form of our religion, but reject its real power.

-II Timothy 3:1-5, The Good News Bible-

I PROTEST

***I** protest* the invasion of our homes by all sorts of men and women through television. Off-color characters whom we would normally not invite through our doors trip across the lighted screen and glue our children to their chairs for hours every day, hours that should be given to wholesome exercise. Dramas of hate and jealousy and intrigues and violence are played out before their eyes. The tangled triangles, the night clubs, the machine gunnings, the sword and pistol plays, the nonsensical comedies come into our intimate firesides to damage and cancel out what Christian faith may have been instilled into the hearts and minds of our children. I protest because children's minds -- and the minds of adults, too -- are so conditioned as to make the abnormal seem normal; the trivial, important; the socially unacceptable, acceptable. Child-slanted advertising turns the child against the parents if they do not buy him the touted product. Super-cunningly devised, super-glamorized liquor and cigarette advertising subconsciously break down resistance and make it easier for boys and girls to slip easily into these habits in the years ahead; why not, they reason, everybody does it! Parents are little aware of the molding power of this communications medium. That there are good programs is not to be gainsaid, but who would say that the good effects outweigh the bad?

I protest the "art model" movie stall, the burlesque show, the stage extravaganzas, the perennial "follies" (how appropriately named!), the barfly, the street solicitor, the private movie, the "adults only" theatre, yes, and even much of the "legitimate stage," together with most of the productions coming out of Hollywood. Some are vulgar, some "refined" and merely suggestive, but the theme is the same. I protest the salacious paperbacks and the "girlie" magazines that are being published by the tons since World War II and brazenly displayed on drugstore and newsstand racks. I protest because the exploiters of the weaknesses of human nature have but one motive -- that of financial gain. What matters it to them that, as the result of their enticements weak men -- and often strong -- find themselves living and moving and having their being in a sex-saturated world! What matters it to these purveyors of flesh that young girls are sucked from their homes into the maelstrom of the gilded life! The brilliant fronts and plush foyers of the movie houses, the colorful paperbacks with their risque' titles, the scintillating dance halls and discotheques, the convivial bars and clubs, the feminine smiles, the red-lighted windows -- do they not all have in common the ultimate purpose of purloining dollars from the pocketbooks of gullible victims! From lone-wolf profiteer to organized underworld syndicate, the traffickers in passion are ensconced in every major city in every country, and through modern communications and transportation media, make their banal influence felt in every community. Sometimes they operate under social censure, sometimes with social approval, but mostly they exist by social tolerance. With what little protest has the modern phenomenon of nudity and undress been accepted! Seaport cities, in particular, are Meccas of sin, and pity the boys of our army and navy who are subjected to the allurements of bars and "joints" with their bevies of beautiful girls and free-flowing liquor. They who do not go along with "wine, women and song" jollity are regarded by their mates as oddballs. Drug and alcohol abuse have become socially acceptable. There is tremendous need for Christian homes that measure up to their responsibilities, as well as for concerted social action against the moral cancers eating at the vitals of our body politic.

INCREDIBLES

Commendable the warning that cigarette smoking is dangerous to health which Government requires in cigarette advertising; *incredible* the multi-billions the companies spend to negate the warning by glamorous ads in newspaper, magazine and television! Commendable the *Reader's Digest* stance against tobacco.

Commendable the billions Christians give for the stilling of physical and spiritual hunger; *incredible* the trillions Christians think they need for themselves to maintain and enhance their lifestyle of the West! *Incredible* the contrast between the Western Christian's worship of God in multi-million-dollar crystal edifice and the third-world fellow-believer's praising of the same God in his thatched-roof mud hut!

Incredible the adult movie house which cities permit and society condones, but *not incredible* the rash of muggings, rapes and child molestations that make first page news! *Incredible*, too, the general acceptance of today's lowered moral standards!

Incredible the worldwide inordinate hunger for wealth, but *not incredible* the resulting poverty, suffering and death! *Incredible* the lengths which individuals, organizations and governments go to hold onto wealth, and *incredible* the multifarious efforts of others to wrest it from them by intrigue, corruption, violence and war!

Incredible the deal which God through Jesus Christ offers to give men what they so much need and want, and *incredible* that so comparatively few accept this fantastic offer! Commendable is the present-day increasing effort by Christians to urge others to see God's once-in-a-lifetime offer to accept it, and *incredible* is Satan's present-day stepped-up effort to keep men from accepting it!

What a world of incredibilities modern man lives in!!

GREYHOUND TRAVELS

May and June 1979

(A number of those I contacted in these travels, as well as others of our friends, may like to know about the details of these various visits. With praise to God for His providences, I share the following experiences.)

With the blessing of my dear companion Eunice, and her manning of our home affairs in Reedley, California, I set out in May of 1979 for a month of travel by Greyhound. Being economy-minded in travel, as usual, I bought thirty days of unlimited travel in the form of an Ameripass for $199.50. A 2,000-mile round trip into Washington State for a speaking engagement was my first excursion, stopping in Salem, Oregon for two days with our son and his family, while contacting other friends.

Returning home, I left Reedley the same day that I arrived. I boarded bus in Fresno at six in the evening for another stint of 2,800 miles to the East. The same bus that I boarded in Phoenix the following morning I disembarked the following morning two days and two nights later in Harrisburg, Pennsylvania.

Just across the plaza from the bus station, which was also the Old Pennsy Station, a Harrisburg landmark, was also as long as I can remember a good popular restaurant, the Alva. Not known to many, the Alva had a few rooms it rented at a very moderate rate. The rooms are not luxurious, but clean. I walked several hundred yards across the plaza and registered for a week at its weekly rate of $30.

Through telephone contacts the following morning, I was taken to Messiah Village, the just-finished multimillion dollar facility for the care of the aged of the Brethren in Christ Church. Since Pennsylvania is my native state, I met again among the 200 guests many of my relatives and friends from Franklin and Lancaster Counties.

It was in this visit with guests Cornelius and Frances Lady, Eunice's brother and sister-in-law, that I was made to realize the gravity of that near-fatal weekend at Three Mile Island. For two days, the 200 guests were checked for their readiness for immediate mass evacuation; each guest was permitted one bag of belongings to take along. Messiah Village is about seven miles from the Three-Mile-Island.

Although I had rather remained at Messiah Village four days instead of four hours, I availed myself of the opportunity to go with one of the Village executives who was passing by Elizabethtown en route to his home. This enabled me to stop at the Brethren in Christ Missions Office in Elizabethtown and to make a long planned for business call. I took Amtrack back to Harrisburg and to my Alva room. This was my first day in Pennsylvania.

The next morning I rode Greyhound 50 miles to Chambersburg, my home town, to visit relatives and friends. That same afternoon I continued on to Washington, D.C. and was able to gain admittance to both the Burundi and the Uganda offices of the State Department of the U.S.A. Here I was able to learn the latest authentic information regarding the two countries about which I've written the books, "No Place To Stop Killing," and "Why Idi Amin?" I was able to return to Harrisburg the same evening.

On my third day, I bussed the 50 miles again to Chambersburg for an appointment, visited Eunice's relatives in Shippensburg, and was back at the Alva by evening. Somewhere along the way that day I picked up the old-fashioned cold bug and found myself in the sneezing and coughing stages. Although there were still contacts I had wanted to make, I had achieved the most important, and that evening I felt it the part of wisdom to "hotfoot it" back home. Accordingly, I boarded bus at 11:30 that evening for Reedley, California.

Whether the Lord was chiding me for asking too much of my body, or He was arranging things providentially, I do not know, but I do know that my return trip home was certainly eventful.

From Harrisburg to Cleveland was not unusual; I had a seat to myself, coughed a little, but not badly. Standing in line for reboarding after our breakfast stop, I became engaged in conversation with a very business-looking businessman. "Believe it or not," he said, "I could not book a flight from Cleveland to Chicago this morning, so I'm having to take the bus." Introducing ourselves, he learned that I am a retired relief worker, while his card titled him as a supervisor for General Electric. Boarding bus, I apologized for not inviting him to the empty seat beside me (He was seated just behind me.), for I did not want to give him my cold. "But I want to talk more with you," he said. I had already given him a copy of "Idi Amin," and he wanted to know more about relief work. At a rest stop, he came to my table with two big dishes of the specialty ice cream which the Ohio Turnpike Restaurants feature, saying, "I know just the right thing for colds." Whether or not his diagnosis was correct, I did appreciate the warmth of his friendship. He said his youngest son had just been graduated and that he had been accepted for his first job. We parted in Chicago. He wished me well for the rest of my trip.

West of Chicago was something else again. For awhile, I occupied the aisle seat, third row behind the driver. But, at Davenport I think it was, a small elderly lady pushed me into the window seat, plunked her imponderables on the seat and floor beside me and maneuvered herself behind the pile, all the while demanding that volunteers put up three heavy paper market bags on the already-filled shelf above. I don't know where space was found for two of the bags, but someone did succeed in stuffing one bagful immediately above us, half the contents of which disgorged themselves on our heads and laps. What seemed like a heavy cut-glass bowl narrowly missed my head. Dozens of color photos were scattered everywhere.

She occupied not only physically the space beside me, but also volubly the air space of the bus from fore to aft. In only fifteen minutes she let it be known she is not a 70-year-old senile woman, that she is going to make a lot of money writing about senior nursing homes, and duly advised all she is going to sue, for ten thousand dollars, a nursing home that did not treat her right. Ostensibly she was talking to me, but I could give only an occasional assent or grunt, for I was busy nose-wiping and coughing in the little space that was left me in row three. This I endured during the night until I noticed a passenger getting off the bus, leaving an empty seat in row four across the aisle. Daylight revealed a woman quite different from that which she proclaimed herself to be -- a pathetic, beringed, nail-polished woman who was desperately looking for recognition and for love. Interspersed between her boastings and oaths during the night were sane strips of conversation which revealed a husband and a family in her life. What furies Satan must have brought down on this woman! He drove her outside the bus at rest stops and sometimes to the back of the bus for her cigarette light-ups. At one of the meal stops, the "hard" lady told me she bought a sandwich for a three-year-old boy whose father had no money. This dulled the sharpness of my estimate of the lady; dare we *ever* categorize an individual before the facts are known? The lady promptly announced her good deed to the driver when he returned to the bus, and to the passengers as they filed in. Later I heard the lady tell the driver she had no money for food; she had spent it on the boy's sandwich. Was it true, or was it bluff?

During the second night at a stop somewhere in the Middle States, a blind young man of maybe 25 and his mother boarded bus and occupied row four across the aisle from me. At the breakfast stop that morning, I was deeply impressed with the devotion of the frail-looking mother for her dependent son, and I responded with an unusual deep sense of appreciation for my own sight. Reboarded again, I was able to make out enough of their conversation to be sure that they were Christians. With an instant finality that had to be of the Holy Spirit, I was impressed to give the young man a copy of my book of conversion stories titled, "I Was Born Again," which I still had with me, and to inscribe the title page as follows: "To my Christian fellow-traveller, greetings! Somehow I have the feeling that you can see more sometimes without eyes than I can with two. God bless you!" For half an hour the mother read excerpts from the book to her son, and then remarked to me, "My son says his own experience agrees with the passages we've just read."

In the ensuing conversation, I learned that the mother-son pair were en route to their home in San Jose, California, and that they were returning from a seminary in Wisconsin from which her son, who had been born blind, had just been graduated. The young theologian said that he is planning for a service program for the handicapped. While the mother was off the bus buying food at a rest stop, I asked him if he understood what I meant by the inscription which I wrote in the book. "Yes," he replied, "I am sure that the Holy Spirit sometimes reveals truths to me which I might not comprehend equally well could I see physically."

We three were still in conversation when a black-bearded, executive-appearing type young man of, I would say, not over thirty asked for the window seat beside me. Our Greyhound had just passed over the border into Nevada and, as I soon learned, my new seatmate was a Nevadan, an official in the Department of Education of that state. He said that his work involved much travel and that he was on his way to Reno. Interestingly, he was not long in half-apologizing for the legal gambling in his state, the Department of Education coming in for a good share from that income. "The citizens of Nevada," he said, "are both liberal and very conservative, and the conservative majority succumb to the pressures of the minority." Our conversation lasted till Reno. By that time he had become intrigued with the type of work which I had been in. "I would like very much to give several years of voluntary service," he said, and requested the address of the Mennonite Central Committee to learn further what fields are currently available.

What variety of friends one makes in travel!

It now became necessary for me to make a decision. The Greyhound schedule which I was riding would put me into Sacramento by evening, and into Fresno around midnight, with a long wait for the morning local bus to Reedley. I learned that I could cut my journey at Reno, and get to Fresno nearer the time of the morning local.

This I decided to do. I wanted to take a good look at one of the incredible facts of American life, the casinos, and to become more aware what a "leecherous" monster Las Vegas and Reno gambling really was. So I spent five hours in Reno going the rounds of the casinos. Those hours were from early afternoon to early evening.

There was a sameness in all of the casinos: Row upon row of slot machines, in almost limitless variations, competing for the player's nickels, dimes, quarters, halves and dollar coins; the grind of spinning wheels which the players were hoping would line up the coveted symbols for a jack pot; a constant din of reluctant machines spitting out coins into tin cups, egging the player on to try for more and more; and almost constantly the voice of the casino attendant announcing over the loudspeaker a winner here of $50, a jack pot there of $200, a really big strike of $1,200 over to the right. "Ladies and gentlemen, the next jack pot can be yours!"

In most of the casinos there were also scattered throughout the gambling halls other games of chance like blackjack, cards, roulette and keno, each gaming group in complete absorption in the game in progress. It seemed to me that on the forehead of everyone could be read the word, "GREED." Indeed, could there be an X-ray taken of the management of the casinos, one could no doubt read the same word in even larger letters!

I watched a housewife-looking woman playing two quarter machines. In a period of about half an hour the two machines netted her about five jack pots. It took two minutes for one machine to spit out 300 quarters (slowly, of course, to make them seem even more!). So many coins was she receiving that she asked me not to let anyone take over the two machines while she went for additional containers for her coins. Her winnings must have totaled over $400. Did I wish I had been she? Yes! But only for a moment; those were worldly thoughts. NO! I would not have taken her place, for such winnings would do Christians no good; our Heavenly Father is richer than all the casinos.

I ended up my tours of the casinos at Harrod's. Whether it was that the machines there paid off better than at other places, the fact is that Harrod's was jampacked. The one-arm bandits were at a premium. The aisles were filled. Hubbub and excitement were at the maximum. The flashing lights, the clinking coins, the self-absorption of the crowd made me feel I was in Satan's very citadel. For twenty minutes I watched a man feed dollars into a big "slot." The giant machine paid off occasionally, but the man at last walked away empty. Losing, not winning, is the *usual* story here. Our own son frankly confesses that for a short period he had been caught up in this glare, and that he experienced winnings - and losses - bigger than anything stated here "In the long run," he says, "you cannot win." He foreswore gambling and has not gone back to it.

I sat in the Keno Room at Harrod's for several games. Although I never played it, I watched the physical drawing of numbers. I've been told it is possible to win up to $25,000 in this game. I then went up to the second floor to Harrod's Restaurant. Here I got myself a piece of pie and a cup of coffee as a sort of fee to sit at the counter to observe high society life . . . the only money I spent in Reno beside a newspaper. Here lounged the elite, eating and playing keno. At every table and from the counter it was possible to see an electric scoreboard of the keno game in progress in the room below. A dozen waitresses checked the players' winnings and issued credit slips for the amounts won.

As I watched, I wondered if this is what one writer described as the place where "kind words were not spoken; only proper ones." Elegantly dressed, overfed ladies munching dainties, sipping drinks and sucking cigarettes, marking their keno cards for the next game great-girthed men making keno their business; waitresses gliding from table to table with food and winnings receipts and gathering up the crumpled keno cards that did not win! Were these what another writer, a columnist, termed "the fat cats" of society who hog . . . and waste . . . their greatly disproportionate share of the earth's blessings and resources? Is it such as these that the prophet Ezekial inveighed against when he wrote (16:49): "Behold, this was the guilt of your sister Sodom; she and her daughters had pride, surfeit of food and prosperous ease, but did not aid the poor and needy?"

The more I observed, the more I was tempted to anger. Did Eunice and I not spend a quarter century bringing aid to the poor and needy of the earth, and was I not here seeing a segment of that high-finance and underworld society that siphons off God's goodies for themselves the while the masses are struggling for the necessities of life? One does not find love for fellowmen in the casinos. The institution of gambling is based on the premise of getting, not giving.

And yet, I had to temper anger with pity. Through the surface excitement of the games I saw boredom written on the faces of nearly all. The life-style of concentrated getting nets diminishing satisfactions. How many of those whom I saw would like to be free from the gambling demon! How many would respond to a concerned presentation of the Gospel? But the casinos see to it tha announcements of fantastic jack pots -- like in the case of Judi Hanson who won $280,000 at Las Vegas on June 10 -- lure the compulsive gambler back to the gambling tables, an abject slave!

It was at the Reno Greyhound that evening that I met the queerest of all the traveling companions on my return home. I noticed him casually while waiting for the bus to Sacramento, a tall, well-built and handsome young man of about twenty-five who sat stiffly in the station, monotonously opening and closing his fists like the jaws of a trench-digging machine. Boarding bus, I forgot about him until, just as the driver was taking off, the young man asked to be seated at the window beside me.

Those were the only words he spoke to me. There he sat, continuing the rhythmic opening and closing of both fists with a frightfully distressing look on his face. "Isn't that a beautiful scene!" I remarked as at sunset we were passing through the snow-covered mountain pass toward Sacramento. He resented my efforts to be friendly, giving the impression he would like to put those claws to my neck.

A feeling of great pity, not unmixed with fear, came upon me and I prayed silently for my seatmate. Here was a sick man. Who was he? What bitterly extreme pressure was he under? The imprint on the portfolio on his lap read, "California State University at Sacramento." Was I sitting beside one of those "normal"people one reads about in the news who suddenly explodes from the pressure of secret hates that send him berserk into society? Has no one noticed this? Does no one care? I can't help but feel that I was witnessing an evident case of demon possession. Just before reaching downtown Sacramento, he stumbled over my feet with such a parting look of hatred as I shall long remember.

Demons are not choosy about the color of the humans they possess. A little black man with a big voice let loose a stream of invective at the waiters in the station restaurant while I was waiting in Sacramento. They tried to quiet him down, but to no avail. Later in the main waiting room, he again railed at two policemen who asked him to leave. They put him out the door onto the street, but he returned as vilely voluble as before. They put him out again, and he returned again. This time, they put on the handcuffs and called the paddy wagon. Why, I ask myself, was the little man not I, and why was I not he? I guess I shall have to wait for an answer to that "why!"

I arrived home the following morning feeling better, I believed, than when I had left Harrisburg. But in a few days my coughing returned. Unwisely, I delayed seeing the doctor, and when I did, he asked if I was able to do nothing. "You have pneumonia," he said, "and will need to take three weeks of bed-rest." I conclude this narrative -- written a few lines a day -- as I'm about to end three weeks of incarceration.

As is so often the case, my illness has been a great blessing. How near the Lord has been to me! How kind Corrine has been in letting us use her home as hospital! How loyally Eunice has stood by me as loving nurse and as proxy for me in a prayer line! And how wonderful the expressions of love and concern of Sunday School class members and others in the local community of believers!

Blessed be the name of the Lord!

Behold, this was the iniquity of thy sister Sodom, pride, fulness of bread, and abundance of idleness was in her and in her daughters, neither did she strengthen the hand of the poor and needy.

-Ezekiel 16:49, The King James Version-

IV
BEYOND HUMAN HELP

* * * * *

CHRIST

THIS ONE THING

The Apostle Paul said, "This one thing I do!"

We -- most of us -- say, "These many things we do!"

The world is full of interesting things these days. There are so many things to do, so many places to go. There are so many ambitions to attain; so many books to read; so many clubs to join; so many programs on the radio; so much information on television; so many people to meet; so many sermons to hear; so many things to eat; so much money to be made; so many instruments to play; so much good to do and so many friends to visit!

Billboards, newspapers, radio and television scream at us with a multitude of voices, "Do this," "Go there," "See what I have!" "Don't miss it!" "You'll be sorry . . . ." Science beckons us into romantic futures; the art world intrigues us by its siren songs; low desire says, "Drink deeply of life's pleasures;" and to the intellectual there stretch ahead vista upon vista of speculative thought. Life is rich, full, entrancing and alluring. Those in whom the fires burn want to hear all, know all, taste all.

And, forthwith, we injudiciously launch ourselves into all the ways of life.

We must have a broad education, we must have culture, we must entertain to the standards of Emily Post, be a connoisseur of "*objet d'art*" and of music, specialists, not in one field, but in many of the sciences and trade and ride into the future with the computer! How we wish we had a thousand lives to pursue a thousand paths! Yes, many things we do!

Saul, the pre-Paul, did this. Saul was tops in everything. None could match his pedigree in his day and one wonders if any could today. He was a Jew, he was Roman, he was a pupil of Gamaliel. He was a lawyer, rich, cultured, self-assured and proud. His zeal was that of a prancing horse. He stretched every nerve to achieve perfection. Well could his motto have been, "Excelsior!" He drank from every fountain. Saul was the near-ideal of the all-around cultured individual that we wish to become.

But that was before Saul met Jesus.

His meeting up with Jesus did something to Saul. It upset him. It changed him. It dazed him. It somersaulted him into a new perspective that was as revolutionary as looking into the big end of a telescope. His former dreams, achievements, heredity and righteousness dwindled into microscopic littleness; Jesus was filling his whole horizon.

From a "many-thing" man, Saul became *the* "one-thing" man, Paul.

The ONE THING gripped Paul, possessed him, filled him and thrilled him. It transformed him. It became his "Magnificant Obsession," and from the nethermost depths of his soul he called out, "I count all things as loss that I might win Christ."

The lesson for us is plain. Our loves and activities must revolve orbit-like around the Magnetic Center -- Christ. "O may it all our powers engage to do the Master's will!"

But seeing Jesus does not mean that the world becomes dull, or that we have no ambitions and activities. We have all learned that we cannot be everything and do everything. Our powers and our time are limited. So life must resolve itself into the constant practice of eliminating the bad for the good, the good for the better, and the better for the best. We are cured of scattermania and smattermania. We do have a singleness of purpose. THIS ONE THING WE DO!

THE GLORY OF CHRIST

Florence Ziegfield has spent a lifetime in what he calls glorifying the American girl. In his huge dramatic productions he has endeavored to exalt the glory and beauty of American girlhood in face and form and synchronization. He has put them in the spotlight, given them magnificent roles, and exalted them to highest dramatic pinnacles.

I have deliberately reached onto the stage for an illustration of the significance and meaning of the word, "to glorify." I think it does give us a mundane example of what it means when one ascribes honor publicly and elevates people to high positions of respect.

Divert now your attention from the stage of the theatre to the great stage of the Universe, and let us view some scenes in the grand Drama of the Ages. On this stage is the spotlight of Eternity. On this stage takes place the glorification of God the Father, the glorification of God the Son, and the glorification of the Believer, that is, you and me.

These are the divisions of my brief message: First, the Father glorifies the Son; Second, the Son glorifies the Father; Third, the Father glorifies the believer, yes, you and me!

Now there is a great activity backstage. In the councils of the eons, before the world was created, God the Father said to God the Son, "I am going to glorify You on the stage of Time." And after the world was created, and man had fallen, God the Son took His cue and came upon the stage of Time. Already at His birth, there was a halo about His head, and from the backstage could be heard the voices of angels as the Father initiated His act of glorification of His Son. The show (pardon the expression) goes on apace. The Son's wisdom in the midst of the learned men; His changing of water into wine; His raising of the dead; His healing of the sick; and His wonderful words were acts leading toward the climax. Particularly brilliant was the scene when the Father's voice was heard from backstage, "This is My Beloved Son, hear Him!" . . . and then later when the Father's great battery of spotlights was turned on the Son at the transfiguration.

Then a second time the Father's approving voice resounds as though from the wings of the stage, "This is my Son in Whom I am well pleased!"

The plot develops quickly. Now the Son is in the Garden. In agony, He prays, "Father, *the* hour has come!" No, the Son is not afraid here, as many would picture Him. I think rather that He is thrilled with exultation, for did He not say over and over, "I delight to do Thy will." And this was *the hour* towards which the Son has been moving since before the beginning of the world. The Son was not a weak and cowardly, pusilanimous victim of circumstances. He was God. He said He could part the curtains and legions of angels would instantly be at His rescue. Even in His death, He did not die as ordinary men without alternative, but He deliberately laid down His life.

Like any plot, it would seem to the onlookers that God the Father was falling short of His avowed purpose of glorifying the Son. The cohorts of the Devil uttered a shout of apparent triumph when the Son cried His last words, "It is finished." The Devil mistook Him as saying, "I am finished." So climactical was the scene that the earth blackened and trembled.

"It is finished!" I like the German rendering of this triumphant exclamation: *"Es ist vollbracht!"* ("The plan of redemption has been brought to completion!") With those words, the Son glorified the Father, and with the resurrection of the Son three days later, the Father glorified the Son, all of which has opened the way for the glorification of all Believers by both the Father and the Son.

It is all so dazzling that it will take all of time and eternity to adequately glorify God the Father and God the Son and God the Holy Spirit for the completed plan of man's redemption.

Did I say "adequately?"

Wrong! The half can never be told.

SATAN

"How art thou fallen from heaven, O Lucifer, son of the morning! How art thou cut down to the ground, which didst weaken the nations! For thou hast said in thine heart, '*I will* ascend into heaven, *I will* exalt *my* throne above the stars of God, *I will* sit also upon the mount of the congregation in the sides of the north, *I will* ascend above the heights of the clouds, *I will* be like the Most High." -- *Isaiah 14:12-14*

In the original harmonies of heaven, there was no place for self will, and Lucifer, the pristine name of Satan, was cast to the earth, where he was to wreak his vengeance on nature and man. "How *art* thou fallen!" says the Prophet under the inspiration of the Spirit. And in the very next verse, verse 15, Isaiah assures the brazen usurper, "Thou shalt *yet* be brought down to Hell!" They that see thee shall say, "Is this the man that made the earth to tremble, that made the world as a wilderness!" Satan has been cast out of heaven to the earth, and he is yet to be cast from the earth into hell, his preordained abode for the rest of eternity.

Satan is to be cast out from the earth, but he is still here. Indeed, it seems he is having his heyday. He has induced and is still inducing multitudes of men to set themselves up against the will of the omnipotent and omniscient God, and the world is chock full of obstreperous and egotistic wills of men who want to try to run the world and to take credit for it.

Witness the Caesars, the Alexanders, the Mussolinis, the Hitlers of history; each wanted to own and to dictate! And witness the lesser lights of history, even down to the poorest peasant; each man having a mind of his own, each wanting his particular way! And witness the resulting chaos and strife in the world: strife within the family, inter-family feuds, church bickerings and denominational fights, racial bitterness, national and international wars, political harangues and gang and criminal violence. What a mess the world is in! And all because the Archangel Lucifer, surnamed Satan, dared try to be equal with God and induced all mankind to follow his lead. "I will be God," shouted Satan in heaven, and a billion echoes resound around the world, "I will be God." Rebellion has spread through the earth, and to an extent never before known, Satan is today indeed the Prince of the Power of the Air.

IRISH FIRES

Spiritual Bonfires Kindled In Belfast By Youth For Christ

It was the last Sunday of the Youth for Christ Congress in Belfast. Since ship passage to England was booked full, I was hurrying about in the early morning empty streets, trying to get a plane booking. Just opposite one of the four big movie houses where flamboyant signs were featuring Gypsy Rose Lee, "the striptease murderess," an Irish lassie of about twenty-five, seeing my Youth for Christ badge, came up to me and said smilingly:

"Good morning, brother!"

"Good morning!" I responded.

"We have been having some wonderful times in our town this week."

"Yes, indeed, we have," I agreed.

"It was a thrilling rally at the Windsor Park Stadium Friday night. God was working."

"Well, thirty thousand at an outdoor rally on a Friday evening and two hundred in the inquiry room is really something to be happy about. Were you there?"

"Indeed, I was," she replied, "and how glad I am that Youth for Christ came to Belfast!" Then reaching out her hand she gripped mine firmly and said, "I surrended last night, gave God my life. I have been praying on my knees all night, and this morning it is settled; oh, I'm so happy!" Joy-moist eyes testified to the truth of her words.

Before I knew it, the had-to-tell-somebody Irish lassie went tripping down the street spilling over with the joy of her newly-consecrated life.

Strangely enough, about an hour later, not far from the same spot, I met a second stirred-up soul.

He crossed the street diagonally so as to get onto the sidewalk a few feet ahead of me. He slowed his steps until we were abreast, then observed my badge with slanting glances. I knew he wanted to talk. We walked together a dozen silent paces, and then he broke the ice and questions came in rapid-fire succession:

"Who are you people? What is the meaning of that badge? Why are you in our city?" His attitude was semi-belligerent, but plainly serious.

"We come," I said, "from many different countries. We are Christians from many different groups, and our common concern is the preaching of the Gospel. You see, we believe that Christ is the only real answer to both the individual's and the world's problems."

"Do you have anything to say about economics?" he asked.

"Not primarily," I answered, " but when a man becomes genuinely newborn in Christ, his business principles become honest and he leaves off unethical practices."

"Well, you people ought to preach an economic program, for the problems of the world are basically economic."

I admitted that there is much inequality, that Christians, too, would like to see things different, but that society cannot be reformed *en masse*; one individual after another must experience a personal transformation of heart; then only can society be changed and social wrongs be righted.

"But Christianity encourages capitalism," he persisted. "The way I hear by the radio and read in the newspaper, the working man is pretty much kept under in America. Christians are interested in getting rich and don't care about the poor people."

"I must confess you have some ground for what you say," I replied. "Many of us Americans are ashamed of the acts and attitudes of some of our fellow-countrymen who call themselves Christians but who nevertheless live selfishly."

"Even here in Belfast," he broke in, "Christians drink and drive sharp bargains and do not care about poor people. I know, for I have lived here all my life. They just are not interested in helping the man that's down and out."

"Yes, one does find so-called Christians everywhere who have no care for the welfare of their fellowmen. They might rightly be called counterfeit Christians. But because this coin -- and I drew out a sterling half-crown piece -- is sometimes counterfeited does not argue that it is not genuine, and because there are hypocrites does not negate the fact that there are genuine Christians, people who give themselves and all they have in the service of God and the welfare of others. I have met many of them, and I believe you have met some, too. They are, of course, in the minority, but one does find true believers and unselfish doers in all parts of the world."

I cited a few examples I had met in my two years in Austria: Helga, the 24-year-old Volksdeutsch refugee from Czechoslovakia who repeatedly risked life and limb in helping others; Pastor Ostermann, in Vienna, who had miraculously escaped a Russian firing squad and who gives the shirt from his back to friend and foe alike; Onkel Doktor Robert, the 85-year-old Arabian prince who had lived with Count Leo Tolstoy and who spent 67 years of his life and a million-dollar inheritance in service to his fellowmen.

"Now there's a great man," interrupted my street companion a bit evasively. "Have you read Tolstoy's works?"

"Parts of them," I replied.

The mention of Tolstoy brought up others of his favorite authors. "I have read," he said, "Tom Paine, Voltaire, and Renan's 'Life of Christ.' Isn't it a pity, though, that Jesus never wrote a book or founded an organization or outlined a social philosophy or established a political party. I think He was a good man, but He gave the world nothing tangible to work on. I am not a Communist, but I think Communism has a more concrete program than does Christianity." Despite his evasiveness regarding genuine Christianity and the chaos of his thinking which these remarks revealed, increasingly I sensed that his attitude was softening.

"How then does one account for the powerful influence which Christ has over men today?" I asked.

"Well, I guess it is some kind of sentimentalism," he said hesitatingly.

"Friend," I said as I secretly prayed for proper words. "I think you have noticed that it is not in me to want to argue, but have we not here come to the basic difference between your thinking and mine; you say that Christ was a good and wise man but one who lacked the organizational ability to establish a strong social and political program that would remedy the world's ills; whereas I believe that Christ is God and that He exercises unprecedented authority and power over matters that have to do with the seat of all philosophies and programs, the heart. The law said, 'Thou shalt not kill,' but Jesus said if you have hatred in your heart it is the same as though you killed. It is a matter of the heart. And that power, like the wind, is invisible, but it is nevertheless real. Jesus Himself said, 'You must be born again!' It is because many thousands of individuals have experienced this miracle of the heart that the influence of Christ is still so powerful in the world today."

Then my friend of the fleeting acquaintance said what I had already guessed:

"For years I have been seeking for the answer to the world's suffering and my own problems. I worry about myself, about my family, about the future, and the worry has brought on stomach ulcers. I am still seeking, and that is why I wanted to talk with you."

Secretly I thanked God for the opportunity to witness; seriously I asked God for wisdom; simply I tried to make plain God's way of salvation; earnestly I pressed for his affirmative decision. "When you go home," I urged, "read and reread the Gospel of John; you cannot help but find the peace of mind you seek if you humbly and repentingly believe." And then I concluded, not egotistically, I hope, but with the positiveness of a witness who knows, "I can truly say that I have found the satisfaction that I longed for, since I accepted Christ as my Savior and Friend; surface storms of a disturbed world do still stir up troubled waves, but deep in my heart there is peace and joy. It is this peace and joy 'which the world cannot give and which the world cannot take away' which I sincerely wish for you."

Our half-hour ended with a firm handclasp and the passing ships continued each on his respective course, possibly never to come within hailing distance again.

Half an hour later I asked a policeman for directions. In friendliest fashion he gave the desired information, and then said, "You are a Christian, aren't you?"

"Yes, indeed," I replied.

"So am I," he responded. "May I walk with you to your address?"

"Certainly," I agreed. And for half an hour an Irish policeman and an American citizen had Christian fellowship on Belfast streets while Youth for Christ rallies were being held in the churches which we passed.

"I'm so sorry I have to be on duty Sunday mornings," he said. "I attend a little mission in the city and know what it is to lead some souls to Christ. Belfast is certainly feeling the effect of Youth for Christ. Churches and unsaved alike are being stirred. Our city has needed it badly. How thankful we are for Youth for Christ!" And in our walk together each told the other what the Lord had done for him.

I think God led me to this policeman, for I had promised my Catholic friend with the stomach ulcer a Bible, and now this officer of the law promised that he would take a copy of the Bible to the address of him with whom I had just spoken. Although we are not helpless puppets in God's hands, it is wonderful to see how God uses one in His wise designs when one lets himself be used.

An hour later and it was 11:30. The plane on which I was successful in getting a booking was to leave shortly after noon. In Belfast, few cafes are open on Sunday; one has to eat in a hotel restaurant. Passing a hotel, I asked a waiter who was standing in the doorway if lunch was ready. "No, not until 12 o'clock," he said. And then, as though a thought had struck him, he urged me to come in. "I will tell the cooks that you must make a plane," he said. He seemed very eager that I come in, ignoring my protestation that I did not want to make him extra trouble.

The reason for his eagerness was soon evident. No sooner had he served me the soup than he bent down and whispered, "I want you to pray for me. I became a Christian last Thursday evening in one of the Youth for Christ services. I do not live with my wife and I want now to be reunited and build a Christian home. All the other waiters here are Catholic and they make fun of me. I want you to really pray for me."

And with every dish that he set on my table, he would whisper additional bits of information. "Some preachers," he said, "come to this restaurant and bring their drinks with them and ask us to serve it with their meals; they are not good examples of Christians." And again, "Some of your Youth for Christ lads stay in this hotel, and they have been talking with me; that's why I made a new start in the Christian life."

When this spiritually hungry waiter brought in the last course, he gave evidence of a living faith. "A miracle has happened today," he said. "I have wanted so badly to go to the rally tonight, but I am always on duty Sunday evenings. A little while ago the manager told me without my asking that I may have off this evening. That has never happened before."

When I walked out of that dining room, my waiter said for the fourth time, "Please do not forget to pray for me." I pass on the request to my readers: let us pray that God may use this waiter to serve the spiritual bread and meat just as he does the material food in his hotel.

What a half-day! Although I was not within the walls of a church that Sunday morning, I had thrills aplenty while walking the Belfast streets. And when I finally boarded the plane for London, my heart was filled likewise in joy and thankfulness that God had permitted me to fan a few of the many bonfires that Youth for Christ had lighted up in Ireland.

JESUS SAVES
A Radio Message

Amidst the blaze of lights in any of our metropolitan cities we can usually see somewhere a sign that proclaims the greatest of all facts in history, the two-word statement, sometimes in neon, sometimes on billboard -- JESUS SAVES!

In these two words we find the Gospel boiled down to its irreducible minimum; it is the Bible in miniature; it is Gospel truth compressed into a spiritual atomic bomb that is capable of disintegrating an old life of sin and of bringing into being a new life that is destined to live forever. It is the essence of reality, the central fact around which all other facts revolve.

You, man there shaving by the mirror, struggling with last night's hangover and disgusted with life, hear those words, "JESUS SAVES."

Young lady at the breakfast table, nibbling your toast with a heavy heart, hear it, hear it, "JESUS SAVES."

University student, you who have been trying to reason out life logically and have found your efforts to be futile, to *you* comes the Good News, "JESUS SAVES."

> We have heard the joyful sound, Jesus saves, Jesus saves;
> Spread the tidings all around, Jesus saves, Jesus saves.

Now what do we mean when we say that Jesus saves?

I would it were possible to divest these words of their triteness and restore to them their pristine freshness and reality.

In the first place, it is Jesus who saves -- and Jesus ONLY. *Jesus* saves. That rules out every other person and every other thing. You must abandon hope of finding satisfaction and joy and eternal life through any means except through the Lord Jesus Christ. I want to relate to you presently some cases of men and women who tried varied methods by which to earn salvation, but who had to give up in despair and fall back on the only name under heaven by which man can be saved. Unmistakably and unequivocably, you must be saved by Jesus if you are to be saved at all.

In the second place, you must be lost if Jesus is to save you. No doubt some of you admit that you *are* lost and that you've tried repeatedly to manage your own affairs but without success. You know you've made a mess of things. You have come to a place where you say that someone must do for you what you have learned you cannot do for yourself. You know you need a savior. Well, you are on a fair way to being saved, for did not Jesus say, "I am come to seek and to save them that are lost?" You must, then, realize indeed that you are lost and that you need saving. Otherwise, Jesus does not -- indeed, He cannot -- save.

In the third place, Jesus *saves*. He really does save. He does a thorough job. His arm is not shortened that He cannot save. He saves to the uttermost. He reaches down to the vile sinner, picks him up, washes away his sins by His blood, forgives him of all his sins, gives him joy and peace, gives him the right to become a son of God and to live with Him throughout eternity. When Jesus saves you, He does a job that exceeds your fondest dreams.

In the fourth place, note that the verb is in the present tense. Jesus saves NOW. Now is the accepted time. There will come a day when the offer of mercy will be withdrawn. There will come a time when it will be too late. But while we are still in the dispensation of Grace, the offer still stands, and Jesus saves any man the moment he acknowledges his sins and asks for forgiveness. Jesus saves now -- TODAY! It is dangerous to put off the matter. Let Him save you *today*.

I recently approached some seventy-five people and asked them to tell me how they were saved. I would like to quote a few of them so that you can identify with them in their lost condition, and then follow in their footsteps of believing on the Lord Jesus Christ for the forgiveness of *your* sins. I shall not mention the names on this broadcast, but I can substantiate every testimony should it be so desired.

The first one I quote you is a Cambridge graduate who describes very vividly his keen sense of guilt and his conversion. Here are his words:

"An evening came when I was quite alone in my room and had prepared for rest. In the usual formal way, I had knelt down for a few moments at the bedside to say my evening prayer. Then without warning, the strong conviction of sin and impurity came upon me with such overpowering strength that every shred of false convention was torn aside, and I knew myself as I really was. To describe the sudden agony which followed is quite beyond my powers. It broke me down completely. There had been nothing during the day to lead up to this. And in church, where I had attended, there had been no stress laid upon conversion as a necessary religious step in Christian progress. It was agonizing, alarming and unexpected, breaking in upon me like a lightning flash followed by its crash of thunder, leaving at first nothing but blackness behind it. I buried my head in my hands and knelt there, alone with God, in an anguish of spirit that blotted out everything else and left me groping for the light.

"So intense was the agony that I was quite unconscious of the lapse of the hours as they went by. So the struggle went on, long into the night. At last a new and wonderful sense of peace and forgiveness came stealing into my life at its very center, and the tears rushed out, bringing infinite relief. I dare not venture to explain further the process of the change that was wrought in me, but I knew at that time without the shadow of a doubt that Christ had won my heart forever. The chain of evil habit was broken, and its hold over me had vanished. As I was walking home, the sunlight was flooding the streets with pure gold and the dayspring of new life had risen in my heart. Christ has become the living Christ to me ever since."

The next testimony is from a man who had been a criminal. Here are his words:

"I was locked up in Leavenworth, in Germany, in England, in Greece and in Egypt. I finally landed in the Massachusetts State Prison in Charlestown where I spent six years. And it was here I was saved.

"One night I was strangely awakened out of my sleep. The Holy Spirit was dealing with me. And so was the Devil. It was a battle royal. The struggle was real, and I realized that I alone had the power of decision. So powerful was the conflict within that I became unaware of the passing of time. I had reached the end of my rope. I got out of my bed, and with nothing to cover me but a cotton nightshirt, I knelt on the cold flagstone floor and said 'yes' to the Holy Spirit. That was the moment when I stepped out of darkest hell into the joy of salvation and life eternal. In a prison house of iron and steel I was delivered from the prison house of sin and Satan. I was a changed man. I was a happy man. I had at last found love. It was not long until everyone in that prison knew that something had happened to me. Oh yes, they made fun of me and laughed and said it would not last. But it did last, and then men began to take notice and to wonder if, after all, I did not have something real.

"Strange as it may seem, the happiest moments of my Christian life I spent in this prison. I had constant fellowship with my Lord. He never let me down. And as He blessed me I passed it on to others. God started a revival right there in prison. Many men were brought under conviction and were saved because I stood true to the Lord. It is marvelous what God can do for an ex-convict on his way to hell. But I know that what God has done for me He can do for anyone who will come to Him and fully surrender."

The next account is that of a country boy who has become one of the country's greatest and best-known preachers. Let us learn how he was saved as a boy:

"One Sunday morning when I was a boy the preacher preached a sermon which I think now was on the subject, 'The Gates of Heaven.' In the sermon he asked us if the gates of Heaven were open right then, would we enter? The question startled me. I knew if the gates of Heaven were opened that day I could not enter, because I could not claim to be a Christian boy. That night the text was 'What shall I do with Jesus?' He said very simply and earnestly that to accept Christ as Savior meant heaven, and that to reject Him as Savior meant hell. I went home that night with the most wretched feeling. I could not sleep. I got up during the night, slipped out of the window that opened on the back porch, and went down to the moonlit watermelon patch. It was a beautiful clear night, and I thought of the heaven beyond the stars and of the hell somewhere in a vast region below.

"At the breakfast table the next morning, my mother said, 'Son, you look like you didn't sleep much last night.'

" 'No, ma'am,' I said, 'I didn't.'

" 'What is the matter?'

" 'I feel awful sinful,' I admitted.

"I had to plow all that day. My misery grew until I finally drove out to the end of a long row and dropped the plow down by the side of Barney, my old white mule. I got down in the fence corner, the corner of an old rail fence, and I told God I felt awfully bad -- awfully sinful -- and that I wanted to be saved.

" 'If one must accept Jesus to be saved,' I prayed, 'then I accept Him.'

"There in the fence corner the Lord saved me.

"That night I walked down the church aisle and let it be known that the Lord had saved me."

That makes three testimonies to the saving power of Jesus Christ: a university graduate, then a criminal who was saved in prison, and I have just finished the story of the young country boy who has since become one of America's best-known preachers. Now here is the testimony of a G.I. who was saved in New Guinea during the recent war. The young man is now in a Bible Institute preparing for fulltime Christian work. Here are his words:

"I was a godless, careless fellow who revelled in sin and iniquity. I knew nothing about Christ except to take His name in vain. I was in the service, and after my preliminary training, was shipped to New Guinea. The first few weeks in the swamps and jungles sufficed to enflame my thirst for liquor and my desire for women. I knew that if I would continue another two weeks like that, my only way out would be self destruction. Religion and church had no place in my thinking, even in these dire circumstances.

"One night, while Japanese snipers in trees were shooting at anything that moved or made a noise, I suddenly realized I was very much out of bounds of army orders. I stood there transfixed with fear. Strangely, an audible voice said, 'Don't be afraid, go forward.' I did, but somehow the strangeness of that voice puzzled me, haunted me. In some unexplainable manner, I associated that voice with God.

"On another day, I casually picked up a scrap of paper. The word 'God' was on it. How very strange! The idea followed me, and grew and grew until one day I decided to go down to the Evangelist-Chaplain's meeting to see if I might find an explanation. And, thank God, that night at the close of the service, I found Jesus as my own Savior. It was the first time I ever heard the Gospel, and as far as I know, the first time anyone had ever prayed for me."

As we read these testimonies, let us remember that they are the words of real flesh-and-blood individuals whom God loves no more and no less than He loves you. And now I want to give you the testimony of an Armenian young man who was saved in Alexandria, Egypt. Hear him!

"I was born not far from the city of Tarsus, the birthplace of Paul the Apostle. I was a lively mischievous boy and skilled in using slings even as David.

"One day, when about ten years of age, while going into the church, I saw in the churchyard the bodies of some seventy-five Armenians who had been slain by the Turks, among them the father of one of my dear playmates. The sight was horrible and the circumstances revolting. A strange feeling of bitter hatred took possession of me, and at that tender age I decided to avenge the massacre of my people. This hatred increased as I grew older.

"At sixteen I became an active member of a socialistic revolutionary organization whose aim was to overthrow the Turkish power as well as Czarism in Russia.

"At eighteen I was compelled to leave Constantinople, so I fled to Rumania. Five of my comrades had been arrested and put in prison because of their revolutionary activities. Three of these young men died from the cruel treatment of the Turks. While in Rumania, I insisted that my father put me in a military school, that I might learn the art of killing men and use it against the Turks. But being so young I was not permitted to enter the military school. I then planned to re-enter Turkey by way of Egypt.

"I had by this time drifted into infidelity and hatred of religious matters through the readings of books of Karl Marx. Strange to say, I took up the study of the Bible in order to discover passages of Scripture that contradicted one another, in order to prove that the Bible is not the Word of God, and thus destroy the faith of my people, whose barbarous persecutions at the hands of the Turks I thought were due to their belief in Christianity.

"While still studying God's Word at Alexandria, Egypt, I became engaged in the cigarette business in order to earn money to pay my passage back to Turkey for the spreading of the revolutionary propaganda. Just a few days before my proposed departure for Turkey, God in His infinite love and mercy, by His Word, spoke to me and showed me my lost condition and the vanity of all my activities, so that I cried, 'Oh, what a miserable man I am! Who shall save me?' This word came to me, 'If the Son, therefore, shall make you free, ye shall be free indeed.' The Word of God searched my heart with power.

"There in the cigarette shop I prayed and accepted the Lord Jesus Christ as my personal Savior and Lord, and the transition was done; I was born again, a new creature in Christ Jesus. Old things had passed away and all things became new. Joy, peace and love began to flood my soul, and instead of desiring to kill the Sultan of Turkey, which had been my greatest ambition, I now prayed for his salvation.

"I immediately left the cigarette business, for I felt that I could not sell my fellowmen poisonous nicotine and at the same time say, 'Hallelujah, I am saved!' I did not even take the wages that were due me, for I felt that it was defiled money. I also gave up the secret organization to which I had belonged, for I knew that Christ only could settle all social and political problems, and I wanted to be wholly at His command. Instead of spreading revolutionary propaganda in the Bible Lands, my desire now was to reach out to these people with the saving message of the Gospel. I immediately began to witness for the Lord Jesus. God honored His Word and saved souls, and we became a little group of believers, burdened for the evangelism of the Bible Lands."

We've learned how Jesus saved a university man, a criminal, a country boy, a G.I. in New Guinea, an Armenian in Alexandria, Egypt. Our last conversion story is that of an American young man who became a well-known Christian merchant:

"A salesman asked me one time to go with him to prayermeeting. There were perhaps two hundred persons present. A handsome old man of about seventy years got up and, in the gravest way, said that he was just waiting for God to take him; that he had lived his life; that God had been good to him; and it was all summed up in the statement that religion was a good thing to *die* by.

"I sat back, and I always had a great fashion of talking to myself. I said, 'Well, old man, you can't touch me. You have lived your life. You haven't any sympathy with a big boy. It has passed over my head.'

"Soon after, a young man got up. He was about 35, and he said:

" 'You have heard an old man tell you that religion was a good thing to die by. I want to tell you it is good to *live* by. I have just begun the Christian life. Two years ago I was converted. I had just begun business, and I had had a prejudice against religion. They told me that a man had to have a face a yard long and could not smile or do anything that would make him happy. You see, I was deceived about that. I am a great deal happier since I became a Christian because it settled things. I am a better businessman. A great load has rolled off my heart, and I can give myself more to my work.'

"I listened to him, and I said to myself, 'There you are. You want to be a businessman. He tells you that religion is good to live by. Another man tells you that religion is good to die by.'

"Then I said, 'Suppose you were in court and heard two statements like that. Would you believe them?' 'Yes,' I replied to myself. 'Well,' I said, 'do you intend ever to be a Christian?' 'Yes.' 'Well, if it's a good thing, why don't you be it right away?' I said, 'Yes, I WILL!'

"I waited in the meeting until everybody went out except the janitor and the old minister, and as he came down the aisle, he met a country boy coming up, and I was the boy. I simply said to him, 'I have settled it tonight to give my heart to Jesus Christ.' And he reached out his hand and said, 'God bless you, my son; you will never regret it!'

"I didn't wait to get some feeling. I accepted the *fact* that I was a sinner, and that there was a Savior for sinners, and I came to Him simply on the proposition that the gift of God is eternal life."

My time is nearly up. I could continue long telling you testimonies like these which I have had the joy of gathering together and editing them for a book which I am preparing. I do not have time to tell you about the gangster who was an alcoholic and got high on dope, using as much as forty grains a day. He tried eight times to commit suicide, but God somehow circumvented his doings by leading him into a mission where he was instantly and completely delivered from all these sins by the power of God. I could tell you about a young lady who was an artist and a model, sketching cover girls for magazines. The Lord convicted her of her sins and she surrendered completely to God, so that now, instead of living in a suite of rooms in the Waldorf-Astoria, driving two Cadillac cars and wearing mink coats, she has given it all up for Jesus' sake and is now working with unfortunate girls in a rescue mission. It is the power of God that transforms a life so completely.

There is one element in being saved that runs through all the stories. It is that of complete surrender to God's will. If you want to be delivered of all your sins, you must want God more than you do your sins. You cannot reserve a pet sin. Christ wants to be Lord of all, or not at all. He wants your will.

Surrender completely to God, and you will find that He will do for you what you have not been able to do for yourself, and what nobody else can do for you. Jesus *does* save if you give him a chance. Jesus saves, and Jesus only. There is no case too hard for Him.

"Him that cometh to Me I will in no wise cast out!" Do come, if you haven't before!

Whoso stoppeth his ears at the cry of the poor, he shall also cry himself, but shall not be heard.

-Proverbs 21:13, The King James Version-

THE THRONE OF GRACE
(A Radio Message on the Mid-Day Devotional Hour Over KOCS, Ontario, California)

Paging everyone who is in trouble! Nobody is barred. Everybody is welcome.

The more serious the trouble, the more reason for joining us, for we are preparing to enter the Throne Room of the Ruler of the Universe. The throne on which He sits is called the THRONE OF GRACE. The more trouble you bring, the more grace you receive. The call is issued in Hebrews 4:16 (Weymouth): "Let us come boldly to the Throne of Grace that we may receive mercy and find grace to help us in our time of need."

More than a few of you who hear are responding, "Yes, I do have a great need." "Yes, I am in trouble."

Come, then, all who seek mercy and grace from God. I, too, am a suppliant.

You, longtime invalid. Days have grown into months and months into years. Sleepless nights have followed painful days. There is *more* grace at this throne.

You, little unwed mother with the crying baby, bring your disappointment and bitterness along into the Throne Room and leave them there.

You, Mr. Businessman, tapping your pencil on your desk, come unload your guilt of ill-gotten gain and come out with strength for future right living.

You, beautiful lady in your fine home and your Cadillac car, come enter the Throne Room to have that persisting void filled.

You say, young man, you've been too bad for God to forgive you. Don't you believe it. "Though your sins be red as scarlet," God says, "they can be made white as snow." There's more than enough of grace for all. Come, join us as we go into the Throne Room.

And your buddies, there, you fellows who've been hooked on drugs, hooked on sex, and are fed up and sorry, come join us. There's plenty of forgiveness with God.

Grandmother with the open Bible, you've served the Lord all your life, and have been coming daily to the Throne of Grace. Come once more and let others note the glow of one who has asked and received largely of the inexhaustible grace of God.

Oh, how many are coming! Before we enter, let us remind ourselves *Whom* we are meeting in the Throne Room. We're going to meet the Ruler of the Universe, God the Father, seated upon a throne, "high and lifted up." The place will be ablaze with glory, and were it not for a second Person, God the Son, seated at the Father's right hand, every one of us would be slain by the insufferable glory and holiness of the scene, not one of us could stand in the august Presence. But God the Son, Jesus Christ, says, "Don't be scared, come right on in." Then as we venture boldly in, we'll hear the Father and Son in conversation:

"Who are these petitioners who dare to come into my Presence?" the Father will say. "Do they not know that I cannot tolerate sinners?"

Then the Son will say, "Do not give double punishment for what these sinners have done, Father. Don't You remember I died one time for all of their sins? You promised you would give a pardon to everyone who would sincerely ask for one."

At this point the Father will ask each one of us who are entering the Throne Room if we really believe that Jesus, His Son, died in our place for our respective sins. If in sincere regret and sincere gratefulness our respective answers are "Yes!" then the Father will reach out His scepter of love and forgiveness, and all of us can make our exit from the Throne Room without our heavy loads and with a burning love for Him Who gave us so great a pardon.

Come, now, pick up your burdens and let us go in. A recording is repeating over and over, "Come to Me, all you who labor and are heavy laden and I will give you rest." Notice the Father's invitation above the entrance to the Throne Room? "Him that cometh to Me I will in no wise cast out!"

Come, then, let us all enter boldly to the Throne of Grace!

HUMAN LOVE
VS
AGAPE LOVE

It is just a story, but it illustrates a point. A fair young man was deeply in love with a beautiful princess. She likewise loved him, but she had a terrible hatred for his mother. When asked for her hand, she consented on one condition, that the young man bring her the bleeding heart of his mother. To satisfy her every wish, the young man did go and slay his mother, and as he came running to her with the bleeding heart of his mother, he stumbled and fell. A cry arose from the bleeding mother-heart, "My son, are you hurt?"

The story illustrates the depth to which human love can go.

But still, it's *human* love.

And Agape love is something else. It is divine love. It has no limits.

Ephesians 4:17-19 (Living Bible): "May your roots go down deep into the soil of God's marvelous love; and you be able to feel and understand, as all God's children should, how long, how wide, how deep and how high His love really is; and to experience this love for yourselves, though it is so great that you will never see the end of it or fully know or understand it. And so at last you will be filled up with God Himself."

And the Apostle Paul bursts out in climaxing superlatives (Ephesians 4:20,21): "Now glory be to God Who by His mighty power at work within us is able to do far more than we would ever dare to ask or even dream of -- infinitely beyond our highest prayers, desires, thoughts, or hopes. May He be given glory forever and ever through endless ages because of His master plan of salvation for the church through Jesus Christ."

That is Agape Love!

WHAT IS YOUR NAME?
WHERE DO YOU LIVE?

The day before Christ's baptism, two of the disciples-to-be were discussing with John the Baptist concerning the Christ, when lo, the Man Himself passed by.

"Behold the Lamb of God," said John the Baptist.

Captivated by His charming words and magnetic bearing, they asked, "Master, where dwellest Thou?"

"Come and see," Jesus replied.

They came and saw where He dwelt and abode with Him.

Another Bible picture:

All day Jacob had been making preparations to effect a reconciliation with his brother Esau, and as night fell, he found his task completed -- with one exception: he must intercede with God, alone, for the success of their meeting. Accordingly he dispatched his whole train -- wife, children, servants, camels and cattle -- across the river, while he himself remained behind, expecting to rejoin them the following morning.

But the unexpected happened that night. An angel appeared to Jacob that night, and Jacob, who recognized in the angel a chance for a blessing, wrestled with him "until the breaking of the day." Nor did the disjointing of his thigh bones cause Jacob to persist less doggedly in his request. This persistence drew from the angel the question, "What is thy name?"

"Jacob," he replied.

And the angel said, "Thy name shall be called no more Jacob, but Israel; for as a prince has thou power with God and with men, and hast prevailed!"

Two beautiful stories, these. But note especially, they contain two rather startling questions: "What is your name?" and "Where do you live?"

Lifting the questions out of their context, let us ask ourselves the same questions:

Where do you live?

The geographical place where you live physically is not so important, although we do recognize that climate and environment have a great deal to do with our lives. It is true that temperate zone industriousness and happiness cannot be maintained in the hotter climates; that German and English pessimism gives way to South European optimism; that the desert plains produce a different type of man than do the well-watered and wooded lands; and that city "nerves" and country solitude contrast sharply.

But that is not the vital point; the question hits deeper. Where do you live mentally? What are the objects of your affection? In your idle moments, should someone rap at the door of your soul, where would they find you? No, not the physical "you," but the inner "you," the self "you." Would you be willing to invite your best friends into your inner world? Where are you living: in a world of hate and envy? in a world of insatiable and selfish ambition? in a world of peace, of purity, of kindly feelings, of thankfulness? Of course, there are physical evidences that show where you are living your life: your facial expression, your general bearing, your library. If on your recreation program is slated movies, the dance, "True Stories" and the casino, your friends will brand you one way; if you are conversant with world affairs, if your Bible is well-worn, if church is on your agenda, your friends will rate you another way. And yet, these are only covert signs; only you yourself know the nature of your true world.

This leads up to the second question: What is your name?

Your living determines your name. A name in itself is hollow, meaningless. It is only a symbol. But every act that you do reads meaning into your name. It is an empty thing to most of the teachers and students when you enter college as a freshman. In each of the four successive years, however, your name becomes more significant, more meaningful, until by graduation day, the world either applauds or hisses at the mention of it. This is true of life itself. It is a serious fact. Certainly no man "liveth to himself." What have you been reading into your name in your life thus far? What do others think of when they write or utter your name? Is your name a community trade-mark for those qualities which are dishonorable, or is it a guarantee of honesty, self-control, aggressiveness? It must be one or the other.

Returning this question to its context, we cannot help but see that Jacob's was an enviable record. Because he had put so much into his name in that night's experience, the angel gave him the more characteristic symbol, "Israel." He was a prince in his influence with God and men. Do you not covet such an appellation? You, too, have the opportunity to make your name so meaningful that God will see fit to give you a more fitting symbol, but --

It all depends upon your answer to the other question, "Where do you live?"

If you want a good name, you must live the life. You have to respond to Christ's "Come and see," and, having discovered the beauty and transcendency of the world in which He lives, you must abide with Him. In no other way can you glorify your name with all that is high and noble.

A Christian who doesn't amount to much in this world should be glad, for he is great in the Lord's sight. But a rich man should be glad that his riches mean nothing to the Lord, for he will soon be gone, like a flower that has lost its beauty and fades away, withered--killed by the scorching summer sun. So it is with rich men. They will soon die and leave behind all their busy activities.

-James 1:9-11, The Living Bible-

YESTERDAY - TODAY - TOMORROW

Those River Brethren barn meetings! Before the time of fancy notes and four-part singing, "Uncle Mart" Oberholzer would *line* the hymn with an unforgettable intonation of voice, and the brethren and sisters, all seated on long benches on the barn floor between the mows of hay and straw, would respond in a unison singing that seemed to fuse the simple spirits into a truly worshipping brotherhood.

It may have been due to the springtime aura that surrounds childhood and gilds people and events, but there seemed to be an openness and a genuineness that wasn't clogged with the appurtenances of pulpit and program, choirs and liturgies. Some senior members of the church sometimes say they miss the warmth and the directness of those days.

My twelve-year-old grandson was sitting beside me in a service in which everything was moving along smoothly, decently and in order. "Grandpa," he whispered, "why does everything have to be so formal?"

Do these appurtenances in a worship service not make convenient media for the true self to hide behind! They make it easier for us to wear our respective respectable masks. We are outgrowing the altar, the confessional. We are becoming the elite, the sophisticated. Soft carpet, soft seats and soft music make us feel really good.

This artificiality carries over into our daily living. The rush of the age is hindering the communion of saints. There is much surface living. Telephone calls end with a thin "thank you for calling." Cleverness characterizes conversations; who can top the last joke? Are we as members of Christ's body so closely knit that we can sing truthfully, "it gives us inward pain when we asunder part!" Is there the warmth that there used to be among our forefathers!

Maybe our youth are giving us the answer. They are telling us we don't live deep where the realities are, that we're professing more than we're possessing. Some even go so far as to use the ugly word "hypocrite."

I attended a Sunday morning worship service recently at which the young people of the church had charge, the preacher sitting in the audience. There was an openness and a frankness that was refreshing!

"Almighty God," they prayed, "we do have Your gift of life and we do want to live it to the full. We admit that within us there are seeds of hot anger, sullen hate, scorn of the lowly, envy of the great. Sometimes we pretend to be what we are not for fear that our real selves are unacceptable. We commit ourselves to activities which we despise. We are afraid. We don't want to cover up the truth about ourselves. We want to be honest with You and with one another. What we want and need is to believe and feel that You love us now. Refresh us and cleanse us so that we won't let our own beauty depend upon making others out to be ugly. Help us to love each other in the name of Jesus Christ our Lord. Amen."

Maybe we adults need to do some unmasking and sincerely cultivate that brotherly concern and neighbor-love that comes from taking our important selves out of the circus ring. Maybe today's youth are showing us the way back to the uncamouflaged sincerity and warmth of our forefathers.

WE ARE CANDLES

The granddaughter of the founder of the Salvation Army, Victoria Booth Demarest, used as a text for an inspirational message the words from Psalms 18:28, "Thou wilt light my candle." She compares Christians to burning candles. The wax, she says, represents the self-centered life; the wick, the soul; the flame, the Spirit of God. God lights our candle through Christ the master candle Who is the Light of the World. The light of the candle comes from its fire and there is no fire without fuel. "Little by little, the wax, which is the fuel, burns away that the flame may keep steady and bright." The writer is saying that brightly burning candles are Christians who are given up to the services of God and fellowmen with such a Spirit-inspired passion as spares neither self nor self-interests.

Most people remain unlighted candles. They want to save their lives. They are for show. Others let themselves be lighted but sputter and flicker in a half-hearted service. Still others are blown out by winds of self-will. Only a comparative few let themselves be used and consumed, and these are the ones who share with Christ the task of lighting the world.

They are a challenging lot, these brightly burning candles of the Lord! Though some are yellow, some white, some black, the colors disappear in the burning and the flame gives forth the white light of the love of God!

I've put this lesson into verse:

You are a candle
on a candlestick;
God's spirit kindles
your soul, the wick.

Your selfish desire,
the wax, is consumed
in the candle's fire,
and it lights the room.

Then do not mutter
when the flame burns bright;
of course it's hotter
when it gives much light.

You're not an heirloom!
It is God's intent
that the flame consume
till you are forespent.

MARIE TRAVER'S DIARY

Marie Travers, a Registered Nurse just out of her teens, signed up for a three-year term of service with a Brethren in Christ mission in Africa. Shortly after her arrival on the field, Marie came down with a fever and passed away within a few days. Her body was flown to her home in New York State. In her room on the mission compound, fellow missionaries found Marie's diary. A paper in this diary contained a prayer, one that Marie had intended only for God's eyes and her own. That precious piece of paper revealed a maturity and a consecration most unusual for a young girl. It follows:

"Anxiety comes when I imagine what emptiness my years here in Africa could bring. Emptiness, not for me, but to those I've been sent to. Lord, forbid! Three years of pleasure, lovely letters home, albums of striking photographs, many meals of roast beef and apple pie and strawberry jam; hours of sewing of Java prints and African patterns; three years of feeding the doggie and cats and making cookies for prayer meeting; three years of keeping a balance between sending tapes and receiving them -- three years of vanity! Lord, forbid it.

"I am asking You to take me these three fleeting years, to pour me out where and when you choose; to help me give of myself unreservedly first to You and then through You to others. May my growing love for Jesus be evident in me. Help me to sow Your seed, or else to water some another has sown. May I encourage instead of criticize, love instead of shun. And now that I've given You these three years, I trust the outcome also to You.

"Lord, I do not ask to become well-known, or famous, for lack of a better word. Let those who have known me forget, as long as they remember You. Forgive me for times I've built an image of myself I'd like others to see. I'm not so holy, I am the least, and yet am what I am because of Jesus.

"I do not know what I may become: a cripple, a widow, perhaps even a wife. I may return home to serve in my parents' house, and once again be a daughter and a sister and an aunt to those I love and left. You may choose to bring me here again, or to another land. And, Lord, I can't forget that You may even come to take me home."

Africa holds the graves of veteran Brethren in Christ missionaries such as Myron Taylor and Bishop Steigerwald, both of whom gave a lifetime of service to the Lord's work there. Certainly they speak loudly of "faithfulness unto death!"

Then there are also graves of those who died early in their missionary careers, such as Harvey Lady, my brother-in-law; Amos Ginder, a former student of mine; and Grace Miller Mann, a former classmate. The recent passing of Marie Traver has highlighted the cases of these youths who were called away soon after their arrival on the field.

I have written the following poem to commemorate the passing of these young missionaries who challenge other youths to complete their unfinished tasks:

CHALLENGERS

Alone and still
on Africa's veldt
they rest.

Torrential rains
have flattened out
mound crests.

Three swarded graves
have challenged all
of us!

We carry on
the work they left
undone.

And now a fourth
has dropped the work
she loved.

They winged her home
to hometown grave
and hoped

that other youth
take up the task
and go

to water seed
that she with love
had sown.

EZEKIEL'S WHEELS

In the first chapter of Ezekiel there is what many regard as a symbolization of the Holy Spirit. Four Living Creatures, each with four faces (those of an eagle, an ox, a lion and a man), move and countermove in straight lines, now in this, now in that direction. A complex of whirring wheels moves when the creatures move and stands still when the creatures stand still. And in the midst of all is an amber-sheened topaz throne, lighted by glowing, diamond-like coals, and shooting tongues of flame. Here is a visible symbol of unseen Reality; here is Life, vibrant, pregnant Life; here is a supernal Beauty; here is Love; here is purged Holiness! And is all this not what the Holy Spirit of the Living God is!

And as the Living Creatures and the whirring wheels thus symbolically visualized in Ezekiel's day the burning movings of the Spirit of God, even so in our day does the Holy Spirit operate dynamically in the lives of real Christians. Whether one's duties lie in the direction of sublime and high tasks (face of the eagle), or in the direction of prodigious labor (face of the ox), or in the direction of danger (face of the lion), or in the direction of plain human living (face of a man), the unseen but all-seeing Holy Spirit moves one enablingly and unswervingly in the fulfillment of one's tasks.

The unspiritual observer sees only the outward; he does not see the fire and the gleam and the glow within. To him a man's goings, comings, and stayings are just a sequence of happenstances, a complex of meaningless movements. He does not know that the truly surrendered believer's steps and stops are ordered of the Holy Spirit, that the movements of a Christian, even in the modern complex living, fit into a pattern of meaningful and divine design.

The believer himself may be only vaguely aware, sometimes totally unaware of the goal toward which he is moving. There are times when he isn't even moving, when the Creatures and the wheels stand still, when there ensue the periods of waiting and seeming no-progress. But the true Christian has *faith*, faith that all things are working together for good. He keeps himself spiritually radar-connected with the Creatures and the wheels, moves in whichever of the four directions they move, and stands still when they stand still. And always for the true believer there is the fire in the midst, sometimes flaming, sometimes glowing, a purging, urging fire "burning in the bones." Content to keep connections intact, he gives over the movements of his being to the direction of the life-impregnating, activating, guiding Spirit of God, the ever-faithful Holy Spirit.

The self-abandoned Christian therefore makes it possible for the unerring Holy Spirit to always lead him in triumph. Be these spiritual triumphs or human defeats, the connected Christian has equal cause for rejoicing, for he knows that wealth and health and scarcity and infirmity are interlaced in a divine pattern that works for his ultimate good and the glory of God. Whereas the doubting Christian wants to know the *why* of life's mixed-up experiences, and complains that the complex "wheels within wheels" do not make sense, the true believer, in marked contrast, is content to "dwell in the place of the Most High," to feel the fire in the midst of the august and loving Presence, to rest his case with the "Divinity that shapes his end," even down to the minutiae of counted hairs. Such is the astounding privilege of the trusting Christian!

The Holy Spirit indwells the church just as He does the individual true believers who compose it. For nearly twenty centuries the Living Spirit of Ezekiel's vision has activated and guided God's faithful chosen band through a vicissitude of experiences that is a conundrum to human thinking. The church has always had its defections, its two-master-serving, so-called Christians, but through the centuries there has likewise also been a modicum of true believers, the real church, which has weathered unshaken all the experiences history has been able to hand it, from baths of blood to overt triumph. And it has been the urging, purging, loving, living Spirit of God that has fired this believing band with its consuming zeal and its impregnable faith. The true church is and always has been totally committed to God and utterly responsive to His Holy Spirit. It is one of God's "mysteries," and the Holy Spirit, "knowing the mind of God," is shaping it for its destined end, a fit bride for its Savior.

In a very special sense, then, the Holy Spirit thus indwells the Christian and the church. But in a larger sense He also controls the whole created world. He is God at work in the world. He is managing all things toward a grand and final climax, and no willful act of man nor frustration of His archfoe, the Devil, can keep the Living Spirit of God from marching grandly on to that final "far-off divine event." The international confusion is but the "wheels within wheels" that are whirring out the detailed plans of Him who makes even the wrath of man to praise Him. Not that the Holy Spirit violates man's will. No, He does not coerce; He entreats and He guides. But He takes the rubble of men's wrong decisions and fits them, together with all events in the world of men and all phenomena in the world of nature, into God's foreordained redemptive plan, and gives purpose and direction to life. God is on His way and He knows where He is going. And the believer is going along, even though he cannot decipher the configuration of the complex wheels that take him. The design of the tapestry is on the underside and the believer will not see it until it comes off the loom.

What comfort and courage all this brings to him who dares believe, who dares give himself completely over to the controls of the all-seeing, all-knowing Holy Spirit! For the believer, life is not a mess, but a message, a message that the Holy Spirit is building His multishaped, multicolored blocks of vicissitudinous experiences, including even the rubble pieces of frustration and suffering, into His eternal heavenly mansion. It is this faith that explains the martyr, that gives the church its vitality in the midst of deadweight secularism. The believer does not understand; he *believes*. But as he believes, glowing coals from the midst of the Living Spirit's amber-sheened topaz throne somehow answer to his faith, and he knows, just *knows*, that all this is true, that God *is* aware of the sparrow's fall.

For missionaries and relief workers -- and this is how this line of thought was triggered -- reliance upon the resources of power and guidance in the Holy Spirit is basic. Without Him our motions are random and ineffective, outside the divine pattern, egotistical, offensive. If there is any class of Christians who need to be on guard against the injection of self-will into its work, it is the full-time servants of the Lord. To walk and to work in the Spirit, to abide in the vine, to keep themselves in the love of God -- this is the only thing missionaries and relief workers should worry about. All other worry is superfluous.

Granted, then, a complete surrender, the servant of the Lord becomes in a limited sense an automaton, a puppet, in the hands of the Holy Spirit. But he is a willing puppet, bound to the Master's hand with cords of love. The Christian of the deeper life is at once the player on the field and the spectator on the bleachers marveling at the Coach's strategy. Viewed closely, a given divine directive may seem devoid of meaning, even detrimental. But with the partial perspective of time and the complete perspective of eternity will come the revelation how vital a part it is in the total picture. And so the in-service Christian lives by faith, and accepts worrilessly and joyfully, if not with complete understanding, the "all things" of God's sending.

What great resources the Holy Spirit puts at the disposal of the trusting child of God! What vibrant life; what multidirectional guidance; what vigilant, sleepless, infinite solicitude; what purging purity; what proferred beauty! The Living Creatures throb just as much today with pregnant Life as in Ezekiel's day; the eye-studded whirring wheels are just as knowing and going; the flames of fire just as purging; the amber-sheened topaz throne just as effulgent with glory; the complex mystery of it all just as awesome! The present age's Holy Ghost bears the selfsame features as Ezekiel's Living Creatures. The vision is for us as much as it was for the prophet.

O living, loving Holy Ghost,
I'd like to be for You a fitting host;
I'd chase away each threat'ning dog and cat,
And place before heart's door the WELCOME mat.

(NOTE: This article was used as the commissioning message in an MCC commissioning service for outgoing workers, among whom were Paul and Doris Janzen Longacre.)

ETERNITY

God called up a man into the vestibule of heaven, saying, "Come thou hither and see the glory of My house." And to the servants that stood around His throne, He said, "Take him and undress him from the robes of flesh, cleanse his vision and put new breath into his nostrils, only touch not any change of his human heart, the heart that weeps and trembles."

It was done! And with a mighty angel for his guide, the man stood ready for his infinite voyage, and from the terraces of heaven, without sound of farewell, at once they wheeled into endless space. Sometimes, with solemn flight of angel wings, they fled through Saharas of darkness, through wildernesses of death that divided the worlds of life; sometimes they swept along frontiers that were quickening under prophetic motion. Then from a distance that is counted only in heaven, light dawned for a time through sleepy film; by unutterable pace the light swept to them; they, by unutterable pace, to the light. In a moment the rushing of planets was upon them; in a moment the blazing of suns was around them.

Then came eternities of twilight that revealed, but were not revealed. On the right hand and the left towered mighty constellations; here were triumphal gates whose magnificent archways rose in altitude by spans that seemed ghostly from infinitude. Without measure were the architraves, past number were the archways, beyond memory the gates.

Within were stars that scaled the eternities below; above was below and below was above to the man stripped of gravitating body -- death was swallowed up in height insurmountable, height was swallowed up in depth unfathomable. Suddenly, as they thus rode from finite to infinite -- suddenly, as they thus tilted over abysmal worlds -- a mighty cry arose, that systems more mysterious, that constellations more glorious, that worlds more billowy, other heights and other depths were coming, were nearing, were at hand.

Then the man sighed and stopped, shuddered and wept. His overburdened heart uttered itself in tears, and he said, "Angel, I will go no farther. For the spirit of man acheth with this infinity. Insufferable is the glory of the universe. End there is none." And from all the listening stars that shone around issued a choral voice, "The man speaks truly; end there is none!"

POEMS

OUR HEARTS IN AFRICA

Two years we lived among the tall
blackskins of Central Africa.
At first the black stood out, but then
they soon became the replicas
of our white friends, and friendships grew,
and when at last the time to part
did come, like Livingstone, we left
our hearts with these dear counterparts.

DISASTER

Tornado rubble, typhoon flood,
quake-shook cities and sliding mud--
nothing of man's material world
makes disaster; it is the swirl
of th' emotions within man's heart
that tears his inner world apart.
Material things? They do not feel!
It is the hurt inside that's real.

WHAT DO YOU HAVE THAT YOU DID NOT RECEIVE?

(Abraham Lincoln's favorite poem was, "Why Should The Spirit Of Mortals Be Proud?" The Apostle Paul, in I Corinthians 4:8, asks much in the same strain, "What Do You Have That You Did Not Receive?")

What do you have that you did not receive,
College Prexy?
Since you're to carry in one cranium
All the knowledge of your curriculum,
You secretly like to let it be thought
You know all about all the things you ought.
O why should the spirit of mortals be proud,
Wearing the color-draped Ph.D. shroud;
What do you have that you did not receive?

What do you have that you did not receive,
Gowned Graduate?
The polished oration won you applause
And you're quite sure it was due you, because,
(Please mark an "X" at the proper place)
You are so lovely (   ), so brilliant (   ), so chaste (   ) --
O why should the spirit of mortals be proud,
Drinking in praise from the applauding crowd;
What do you have that you did not receive?

What do you have that you did not receive,
Woman of Wealth?
Contrast your house and its tangible glut
With millions of windowless African huts.
Instead of selfish and inbred living,
Let there be outgo of deep thanksgiving!
Why should the spirits of mortals be proud;
Does wealth give the priv'lege to act highbrowed?
What do you have that you did not receive?

What do you have that you did not receive,
Big Businessman?
Little by little you've achieved success
Until successes demand excesses
Of effort and strength -- and yet you keep on,
Too proud to injure your success icon.

Why should the spirit of mortals be proud;
Why should your pride in casket enshroud?
You are asking for more than what you received.

What do you have that you did not receive,
Wielder of Pen?
God gives you insight and your heart is stirred
And forthwith you put the thoughts into words.
With beauty and strength words flow from your pen,
And then you expect the praises of men.
O why should the spirit of mortals be proud;
Why should praise-hunger God's message becloud?
What do you have that you did not receive?

What do you have that you did not receive,
Missionary?
A missionary is one who is sent
To bring Good News to a world in ferment;
Does being God-sent make necessary
Th' aggrandizement of the emissary?
Why should the spirit of mortals be proud:
It's better the messenger's head be bowed.
What do you have that you did not receive?

What do you have that you did not receive,
Man of the Cloth?
"I want to be a spiritual leader;
To be, indeed, an anointed preacher!"
But under the vest, inside the breast,
There is secret desire that *I* be best--
O why should the spirit of mortals be proud?
E'en preachers must talk with God in the cloud!
What do you have that you did not receive?

We do have nothing we did not receive,
O Fellowmen!
God gives us body and He gives us breath,
And everything else between birth and death;
Incongruous the air of us who declare
That we need no helper from anywhere!
Why should any of us mortals be proud?
Let's get on our knees and confess aloud
That we're big-headed, pig-headed, proud!

TO US THE HAVES

Count your blessings.
They do!
They see
our possessings*
and wish
they had
just half of what
we say
we need--
we overfat!

Dare we pursue
our good living,
ignore the queue
of poor
and the
injustices
they bear
from man's
base devices?

Let's share our plus--
our things
ourselves!
Be venturous
and find
the joy
of filling up
another's
longtime
near-empty cup!

*The term "possessings" is used as a noun to picture a things-hungry individual pursuing "the good life."

THAT HOUSE BY THE SIDE OF THE ROAD
(with apologies to Sam Foss)

There are hermit souls who live withdrawn
In the peace of their self-content;
There are souls ingrown, without a care
For a neighbor improvident.
"It's *my* life I am living," they say,
"And who should there be to decry
When I want to be left alone and
Let the rest of the world go by!"

These are the few who have their abode
Far back from the highway of life.
But most of us build along the road
Where go men who are faint with strife,
And we aim to help the passersby--
The sick, the scared, the destitute,
Even some who are about to die--
When it does our convenience suit.

We are so busy with our housekeeping
In the house by the side of the road,
We really have little time for weeping
With travelers with a heavy load.
It is such a joy their welfare seeking,
If only there weren't so much housecleaning!

For only a few can we therefore share
The tithe of our time; it's all we can spare.
All the others who pass must go elsewhere,
For mustn't we keep our house in repair!
And yet we do know from the Sacred Tome
Jesus our Lord had no persn'l abode;
Our Master had neither a house nor a home;
He gave *all* of His time to the crowd in the road!

FROM ZION TO LION

In this poem, Sydney Lanier's "Song of the Chatahoochee" and the story of the Mount of Transfiguration are used to advance the thought of service in hard places where the need is greatest. The title derives from the thought of "Zion" as a place of worship, and of Satan, who is spoken of as "a roaring lion." Lanier, in his poem, personifies the waters of the Chatahoochee River and has it being implored by the stones and the trees to remain up in the cool mountains and not go down into the hot and humid valley. But the stream continues on its way. The poem was read at an MCC Commissioning Service for personnel being sent forth to serve "in the name of Christ."

Lanier
Made thrones from stones
On mountain cones;
Urged crystal waters to postpone
Their foaming flight down mountainside
Where they'd with many things collide,
And begged instead the waters glide
To shady pools, and there abide
Securely in the airy freedom
Of th' elysian mountain kingdom.

Peter
Wanted to stay
Many a day
On Transformation Mount and pray,
T' wander about on holy ground.
He, thrilled, exclaimed, "Good to be here;
Why can't we all stay here all year;
With God and prophets tabernacled
We're here from menial care unshackled!"

Lanier,
On *second* thought,
Said th' waters ought
Not linger long on th' enchanted spot,
Not laze around, and lave and lap
The pebbly gems, and make a lap
Where fish and butterflies can play
In a perpetual holiday.
'Tis fine, he said, but all the while
The plains below remained sterile.

Peter,
Alas, found out
About the drought
Of faith in plain below; no shout
Of vict'ry there! The while he saw
The heavenly display, the claw
Of Lucifer did tightly hold
The lunatic. How sad, behold,
Had not the glory been turned off!
The lad had died, and crowds had scoffed!

Jesus,
'Tis true, did say
To stay and pray
Till Pentecost, but then--aweigh
To Greece and Rome and all the world
Where heathen opposition swirled!
He meant that they should stay to go,
Should stay just till they caught the glow;
Then with sheer negligence to pay
Should go and "throw their lives away."

I
Often ponder,
Sometimes wonder
If I'm making bigger blunder
Than did Peter (Lord, your pardon
That I hang so much 'round Zion!)
Two hundred times within the year
I go to church to see and hear
About the glories of God's grace
And seek to better know His face;
To heaven to raise my heart and eyes
And for the masses "sympathize."

But can I count e'en just two times
When I've forsaken church and chimes
To soil my suit on dusty plains
Where men are suffering demon pains!
You see, I'm not *really* sorry!
Much too well I like the glory
Of the Holy Sanctuary;
My "love" is so visionary!

I do, of course, my off'rings bring,
Wholeheartedly join in to sing
"Praise God from Whom all Blessings Flow,"
But seldom with the blessings go.

Unheedingly, unseeingly,
Sequestered in the quietude
Of high Mount Zion's solitude
I praise my Lord and Master loud,
Far up above the rabble crowd.
I praise Him, but do not share my Lord;
Him to myself I selfish hoard.

Satan
Meanwhile passes
Through the masses
In the valley, and harasses
Unrelentingly the helpless,
Dusty, thirsty multitude
And brings them into servitude.

Lord,
Are You my Lord?
Really my *Lord?*
Too, other Christians call You "Lord!"
We all call You "Lord and Master,"
But -- the world is near disaster!
Believers sit around the hearth
And in the valley there is dearth;
We do limit You to cloister
While the social sores foul fester!
Lord, is it this aridity
Of faith and fruit, this nullity,
What's wrong with Christianity?

Lord,
Help us to leave the mountain tops
And go to farm the valley crops!
Bestir us from our "ease in Zion,"
And send us down to meet "The Lion!"

INSENSATE

Two donkey hours away
From Zion City lay
A beaten man.

Levite and Priest espied
And heard the man who cried,
But passed him by.

A few jet hours away
From San Francisco lay
More sore-beat men.

We fly too high to hear
The cry and see the tear--
We eat our lunch.

POSSESSIONS

At first we possess our possessions,
But with the increase of accessions
To our possession, prepossessions
Of ownership become obsessions--
And we're possessed by our possessions

THE CRY

I heard it cry and cry and cry
throughout the night. Didst ever try
to sleep the while a child did cry
a plaintive, hours-long midnight cry?
If so, did you thereby descry
the larger universal cry?

ENNUI

If man remove
from repertoire
of his beliefs
hope, love and God,
and substitute
existentialism,
agnosticism
and nihilism,
man falls apart!

For him there is
no "good," no goad
to worthy goal.
He's like the cow--
just eats her food
and chews her cud--
life passes by.

Impress'nst art
architectur'l junk
meaningless verse
and down-beat rock--
they all bespeak
the bleak inside
of moral-less,
rudder-less man!

GOD ON THE NIGHT SHIFT

When on my bed at night
The whirring wheels go overmuch,
I sometimes then recite
Such promises of God that touch
On *needless* pressing care.
And then I feel God still the wave,
See Him my burdens bear;
He the Pillar; I th' architrave!

WHAT IF . . . . . . ?

Tiniest gnat!

You are disporting yourself on the white
sheet of paper under my desk light.

I cannot make out your parts, but your eyes and legs and
wings must be perfect, for you alight and realight
as though filled with a dancing glee.

And you are aware of me; when my hands move, you move.

But you are annoying me a good bit.

Aha!

I was quicker than you that time!

I wipe the speck from my finger.

But somehow I cannot wipe you off my mind; in size you
were to me as I am to God. I think I have often
annoyed Him, like you me;

What if . . . . . . ?

BETHLEHEM

Behold the Baby! Aye,
without His aid
was nothing made
in earth, in sea, in sky!

To think! He made the earth!
and you and me!
Come close and see!
God in His humble birth!

"Immanuel" we sing!
Hallelujah!
"Immanuel" we shout!
Hallelujah!

I LIKE LIFE SMOOTH

I like life smooth
And in a groove
And all I do be flesh-approved.
On Beautyrest to roll and loll
While music soft lulls weary soul
To tranquil calm; then to cajole
Sweet sleep, bid her to me caress
Into complete unconsciousness.
I like life smooth
And in a groove
And all I do be flesh-approved.

I've often wooed
The gourmet's mood
For dainty, rich, exotic food.
How right the whole world seems when you
Take in your hand a long menu!
Both table d'hote and a la carte
Intrigue, and make the water start.
Then leisurely to dine and wine
From silver plate and earthen stein
In atmosphere lush and refined
Does magic-like create, I find,
A psychological feeling
Of a physical well-being.
I love the gastronomic mood;
It hums the body's sweet 'etude!
I like life smooth
And in a groove
And all I do be flesh-approved.

Behind the wheel,
In shining steel
Deep-plushcushioned, I like to feel
the lazing motor spring to life
At touch of toe, and then to knife
The air in smoothest power-glide.
In front, beneath, and at my side
Are gears and gadgets that preside,
While all I need to do is guide
The automatic-powered wheel
And watch the silent miles unreel
The countryside.
I like life smooth
And in a groove
And all I do be flesh-approved.

I try to foresee,
And thus to flee,
Whate'er might bring on tragedy:
Insure my house and things 'gainst fire;
Take out Blue Cross as pacifier
For fear of body-suff'rings dire;
Insulate my house for heat and cold,
Seeing I'll soon be getting old;

Stock well my cabinet 'gainst pain
Of fever, poison, cut and sprain.
So by foresight I wise forestall
Right many ill, some big, some small,
Which pleasant flesh so painful maul.
I always like the surety
Of physical security;
I like life smooth
And in a groove
And all I do be flesh-approved.

I quite approve
Whatever move
Does tend to make religion smooth:
Remodelled church and vested choir,
Inch-thick carpet, carilloned spire,
Prismed windows and cushioned pew,
Lighting effect of sky-blue hue--
All such details neatly cohere
To make a sacred atmosphere
In which to worship God and pray
For strength to meet the coming day.
To be with friendly handshake greeted,
And in my 'customed pew be seated;
To hear the organ's soft prelude
Call me to restfully exclude
All mundane thoughts; to lowly kneel
On cushioned stool and there to feel
The organed choir and chimes inspire
My wearied soul and raise it higher
Than e'en the church's airy spire
Till it, too, plucks the heavenly lyre--
Ah, this is worship ideal!
And when the pastor takes his stance
And opens up such vistic glance
Of the unbounded, bright expanse
Of love of God, my heart does dance
And soar still high'r on wings of dove
In contemplation of this love!
What a discordant, jarring note
'T would be to here inject and quote
Rude passages about hellfire
And speak of God as having ire!

No, no, I much prefer, forsooth,
The Sunday services to soothe
The pinpricks of the week, and feel
To live take on a fresh appeal;
I always like the theme of love
To lift my thoughts to realms above!
And grand-built sanctuary
Makes worship voluntary!
I like life smooth
And in a groove
And all I do be flesh-approved.

Command those who are rich in the things of this life not to be proud, but to place their hope, not in such uncertain things as riches, but in God, who generously gives us everything for our enjoyment. Command them to do good, to be rich in good works, to be generous and ready to share with others. In this way they will store up for themselves a treasure which will be a solid foundation for the future. And then they will be able to win the life which is true life.

-I Timothy 6:17-19, The Good News Bible-

POSTSCRIPT

She was Czech. She was twenty. Her father, a brilliant university professor, embraced Marxism and defected to Russia. Her mother had earlier taught French in a private girls' school in London. Came then the two invasions of Czechoslovakia, first the Hitler forces and later the Russians. Mother and daughter were divested of their fine home, and turned up as refugees in Vienna with only the clothes on their backs.

We met them there in 1950. Brilliant like her father, she spoke Czech, German, French and English fluently and some Russian. Sensitive like her mother, she identified with the poor and suffering. Almost instantly, she became an adjunct to the MCC in the Danubian city. She served as interpreter, not only of language, but also of European mores and the current situations.

Herself destitute, she often passed on to Iron Curtain refugees the aid which we had intended for her. For nearly two years, she gave herself unstintingly, empathizing with helpless people in direst circumstances. "Once you start helping someone," she said, "never let him down." To detail the ways she carried out her own advice would require a second volume. The memory of her self-giving has been a constant challenge to us.

Today, July 11, 1980, twenty-eight years after our farewell in Vienna, we received a letter from her in Upper Volta, West Africa. It is the last of a hundred letters that have bridged the years between. Whereas the years following took us to Japan, then Hong Kong, and then Africa, they took her directly to Africa where she earned a Doctor's degree by researching the history of the Fulanis, the cattle-raising people throughout the grassland areas of West Africa. Running true to character, she identified with the people she was writing about to the extent that she became one of them, marrying a Fulani native of Upper Volta.

There, on the rim of the notorious Sahel, she has been aiding and suffering with her people against the encroaching Great Desert. Whereas she and her husband live a bit south of the rim, her daughter-in-law lives farther north *in* the Sahel area, and the letter we received today has to do with her visit to her daughter-in-law on the occasion of the birth of their second child, Ifo.

"Dear Papa and Mamie," she handwrites at the top of her typed letter, "these are some impressions from the Sahel, which I visited in April. My husband's family live there. It is not possible to describe the misery. The desert advances. The heat is horrible. Until now I haven't quite recovered." Then follows her classic description:

Wherever you look--there is sand, whirling, dancing, stretching to the horizon, a waving, glowing blanket. Giant Baobab trees are lonely guardians of the Sahel. Life is ebbing out.

Eighty years ago, antelope and elephants came through the dense forest to a roaring river. Today reigns the solitude of stinging heat. There are neither mosquitoes nor bees, only a lonely vulture turning his eternal rounds in a blazing sky. There is no longer any grass under the hoofs of the meager cows. Water, isn't there any water?

My foot touches a skeleton which the wind has brushed clean, a ten-year-old boy. Near the pile of bones are relics of the Ston Age: pottery, stone adzes, grinding stones. Thousands of years ago this was a densely populated country, negro drums echoing across the river.

Then one day came the light-skinned Fulanis.

During the endless migration of these Fulanis throughout the black Soudan among fetish worshippers and trance-dancers, they developed an iron mold of self-discipline, and this discipline has greatly shaped their character.

Today, hunger and thirst are their companions. Misery is their daily bread. The glowing wind of the desert sucks the marrow of men and animals. Epidemics rush across the plains.

Khadija, my 20-year-old daughter-in-law, opens the door, smiling timidly.

"Do you know it?"

"Yes, I do," I reply. I do my best to speak calmly.

In the night when little Samba was born, Khadija had remarked, "It hurts, but it's ridiculous to cry." Now, she just says, "Ifo didn't want to stay."

"Forgive us, daughter, for reminding you by our presence that your little son has left you forever."

No wonder that Ifo didn't want to stay at the dry breast of his starved mother! He escaped from the claws of suffering.

The project, "Green Sahel," is planting trees. Gardens are supposed to be irrigated....so many things are supposed to happen!

When?

Meanwhile, well-nourished "development-aides" tell each other amusing stories, and white experts feast on enormous salaries, celebrating Africa's funeral!

And Ifo's.

She ends with another handwritten note: "We hope you'll have a nice summer vacation--surely with your children and grandchildren? Lots and lots of love!"

He shall judge the poor of the people, He shall save the children of the needy, and shall break in pieces the oppressor. For He shall deliver the needy when he crieth; the poor also, and him that hath no helper. He shall spare the souls of the needy. He shall redeem their soul from deceit and violence; and precious shall be their blood in His sight.

-Psalms 72:4, 12, 13, 14; The King James Version-